THE KING AND HIS SHADOW

THE KING AND HIS SHADOW
The Autobiography of Albert A. Coates

Albert A. Coates

Edited by Stephanie D. Forman

The Book Guild Ltd
Sussex, England

This book is sold subject to the condition that it shall not, by way of trade or otherwise, be lent, re-sold, hired out, photocopied or held in any retrieval system or otherwise circulated without the publisher's prior consent in any form of binding or cover other than that in which this is published and without a similar condition including this condition being imposed on the subsequent purchaser.

The Book Guild Ltd
25 High Street
Lewes, Sussex

First published 1999
© Stephanie D. Forman 1999
Set in Times
Typesetting by Southern Reproductions (Sussex)
Crowborough, Sussex
Printed in Great Britain by
Bookcraft (Bath) Ltd, Avon

A catalogue record for this book is
available from the British Library

ISBN 1 85776 300 9

CONTENTS

Introduction	ix
In the Front Line	1
On the Beat	14
Special Branch	31
Spies and Subversives	44
The King and I	58
The War Gets Worse	69
Visiting the Famous	82
Royal Occasions	96
Scotland the Brave	110
Manoeuvres	123
The End at Last	134
Guests of the King of Norway	146
New Life in Canada	154
Home Again	167

In memory of the bond that existed between Norway and England during the World War II years, and which continues to this day; also to my father's colleagues who worked alongside him at Scotland Yard; and to the Norwegian friendships that were made and still exist, especially with Per Winther Leversen and his family.

S.D.F.

INTRODUCTION

Albert Victor Sealey Coates
(King Haakon VII's Shadow – 1940–45)

My father wrote his autobiography between the years 1954 and 1955, requesting that I, his daughter Stephanie, arrange to have it printed in book form with copies to each of his grandsons.

This request was accomplished in the years 1988 through 1990.

My father was born at Hythe, Kent, England, on 22 January 1898 – one of four brothers and two sisters. He enlisted in World War I in 1915 at age 17 and served with the Royal Artillery in France throughout the hostilities, ending 11 November 1918, and received his honourable discharge on 19 May 1919. He applied for and was accepted into the London Metropolitan Police Force on 8 September 1919. On 6 June 1927, he was appointed to the Special Branch of the CID connected with crime against the state – with particular duties regarding the safety of the Royal Family, visiting heads of state and government members. He was married on 6 November 1919 to Clarice Gladys Beatrice Hawkins, leading a beautiful and happy life for 59 years. During this marriage, there were three children – two sons, Donald Albert and Arthur Albert, and one daughter, Stephanie Doreen.

Shortly after the beginning of the Second World War, Hitler invaded and occupied Norway. King Haakon VII and his son, the Crown Prince Olaf, left Norway to set up their Government in the United Kingdom. The rest of the Royal Family proceeded to the United States under the protection of the US Government.

My father, now Detective Sergeant CID, was appointed the personal bodyguard to King Haakon VII of Norway serving the King for five years – 1940 to 1945. The King would often say that my father was just like his 'shadow' during this period – always with him!

During my father's tenure as the King's bodyguard, there were many periods of discussion between them covering their respective families, world affairs and, in particular, the countries ruled by Communism. This relationship resulted in my father and the King becoming very close friends and the friendship continued after the King returned to Norway. Shortly thereafter my father and mother received an invitation to spend their vacation period as the King's guests at the Summer Palace in Oslo. After the King returned to Norway in 1945 a personal correspondence was maintained and many letters were exchanged between my father and King Haakon. The letters from the King were handwritten on royal stationery. This exchange of letters continued from 1945, when the King returned to Norway, until his death in 1957 and included the period my father and mother moved from England to Canada in 1947 to be nearer their children and grandchildren. My father and mother spent seven years in Canada before returning to England for personal reasons.

My father lived several years after completing this book. He passed away in June 1978, just four months after my mother's death.

King Haakon VII gave my father gifts during their relationship, including two sets of cuff links; one set gold and the other gold and platinum, and a silver cigarette box – all of which were engraved with the King's crest.

In addition to King Haakon VII, my father was also

assigned to protect Mr Cordell Hull, the United States Secretary of State. This assignment was in 1933 while Mr Hull attended a monetary conference during a visit to England and, as a result, he and my father became close friends. In appreciation Mr Hull gave my father a personalized photograph and an engraved silver cigarette case.

Stephanie D. Forman

1

In the Front Line

In the early hours of 22 January 1898, I first saw the light of day. As far as I can gather from subsequent conversation, I was not at that particular time very welcome. Times were bad and an extra mouth to feed tended to strain the family exchequer. Still, I gather the household at Prospect Place, Hythe, where we lived in those days, was not unduly perturbed and life continued on in a normal way. The earliest memory I have of my childhood days is the frequent visits of an old friend of my mother's. She was a spinster and apparently loved to bathe the kids. Apart from these little ceremonies, I can remember very little of those early days. Perhaps that is as well, because my mother assured me life was very difficult and amusements few and far between. Thanks to a more enlightened world, with all its modernization, life is much more tolerable today.

When I was eight years of age, as was common with kids of those days, we loved to do some small task in the household before leaving for school. After school, another small chore was accomplished, together with homework and then to bed at between 7 and 7.30 p.m. Compare these times with the ultra-modern generation of today. We were all proud to be part of the household. Sunday was a day of rest and meditation and devoted to religious teachings. It was church in the morning, Sunday school in the afternoon and church again in the evening. For a period I was a choirboy and received the magnificent sum of one farthing for every practice. I often wonder if all the time we devoted to church ever was worthwhile. I have long since come to the conclusion that real Christianity is kindness to one's fellow man.

My schooldays were not very distinguished. I was an average student and managed to pass my yearly examinations without too much effort, but never brilliantly. One outstanding incident in my early life was the winning of a competition in which all the pupils of schools in Hythe and Folkestone took part. We were asked to write an essay on 'The British Empire'. The results were to be announced on 24 May, a school holiday in those days. On this particular day I had won two minor prizes in sports, but strange to say, I was not in the least interested with them, my thoughts were centred on the prize for the essay. I had a feeling that I had won the major prize, and as a consequence, was not surprised when I heard my name called as the first prize winner. I was of course overwhelmed with joy and still look upon that day as the proudest one in my life.

As boys are wont to do, we played frequently on an old hulk on the canal. Warnings from our elders were of no avail. This was unfortunate, because the inevitable happened. One of our number fell off the hulk into the water, and before he could be extricated from the weeds, he was drowned. I remember still the sad procession around the coffin.

Sport never captured my imagination enough to enable me to become proficient. I took part in many games, but seldom excelled in any particular one. My younger brother Ted became a footballer of outstanding ability, and was the idol of the school.

One day in 1909, we heard that a Frenchman named Blériot had landed in Dover after having flown the Channel. We promptly got out our bikes and cycled away to Dover – covering the 15 miles in good time. It was a momentous occasion for us all. On the return journey, my brakes failed on the notorious Valiant Sailor hill; somehow I managed to steer a straight course and toppled over at the bottom of the hill, with barely a scratch, but my bike was an utter wreck.

Shortly after this, there was an air display at Westernhanger Racecourse. It was most thrilling to observe men flying mere pieces of canvas tied together with string, or so it seemed to us. It hardly seems possible that those machines were to be the forerunners of the magnificent planes that travel to the far corners of the world today.

At the age of 12 years, I began to dream of life in the future, but owing to the impecuniosity of my youth, my boyhood dreams were never realized. After leaving school, I tried various types of occupations, always with the hopes of adventure in the great outside world, but with very little success in those early days. My first job was in domestic service. I had an idea this would lead to travel. I was really thrilled when I boarded the train on my way to the new post. Up to then, the farthest I had been from home was on the infrequent trips to Folkestone and Dover. This journey of 65 miles was my first great adventure. Unfortunately, I was not the hero I had imagined myself to be. When I heard the church bells chiming on the first Sunday away from home, I became terribly homesick and by the end of the first month was back home again. I was ashamed, but soon reconciled myself by accepting a similar job nearer home. After several months of this type of employment, I came to the conclusion that my chances of travelling had not been increased. So my thoughts changed to a different sphere of employment. Nothing new about this, boys are always changing their minds – even today.

With my parents' approval, I became an apprentice to printing with a local newspaper – it was a local 'rag', but nevertheless I had at last made a good decision. My main interest was to gather news, but of course I had to start with more mundane tasks. I became what is commonly called a 'printer's devil', and for a start, I really was one. I was out for a bit of fun at the least excuse. Frequently I was checked for larking about, especially because most times this led to 'pied' jobs. One day I was throwing ink at one of my colleagues, but unfortunately it hit the foreman. This little episode nearly ended my career as a printer, but the foreman was not the ogre I had pictured him to be. He gave me a good telling-off, and from then I set about my task with earnestness and became very proficient, especially in display work. So much so, that I was soon performing these tasks without any supervision. The praise I received prompted me to study this branch of printing with more zeal, and I used my spare cash to further my studies. Quite an effort, considering my remuneration was only 2s 6d per week, plus a few shillings for work I did at home. I attended evening classes on three nights a week and was also a member of the Boy Scouts. Up to early 1914 I had been unable to go to camp owing to lack of funds, but this particular year, I was able to go on conditions that I took my younger brother, Ken – a mere kid of six summers. Also at the camp was my other brother Ted. He was a very popular member of the troop and was a drummer in the band. We trekked to camp, a mere 20 miles from home.

Towards the end of the camp, we heard of the declaration of war against Germany. Our Scoutmaster, who was our teacher at school and a member of the Territorials, was called up for service direct from camp. Several weeks later he was killed while at bomb-throwing practice. Like many boys of that time, I was anxious to do something practical in the war. I tried to enlist in the local Territorials, but was prevented from doing so by my dad. He did, however, give me permission to enlist in a new branch – the Royal Naval Air Service – but I was at that time very friendly with a local lad who, being a year older than I, was not eligible to join this new unit. Under the circumstances I decided to wait for a while.

Shortly after this, Mother persuaded my dad to transfer from the School of Musketry to the Military Academy at Woolwich. He had been ill for some time, and she mistakenly thought a move to London would be of benefit to him. The move was not a success, because Dad died shortly afterwards. I think the change of surroundings, which were far from congenial, hastened his death. We had to live in crowded conditions, because Woolwich at that time was the centre of armaments production. The Commandant of the academy offered my mother a job as housekeeper to the chaplain. We moved into spacious quarters, and apart from the sadness at the loss of Dad, whom I had always considered a pal, we were very comfortable. I had already obtained employment with the local newspaper office. The main topic of conversation at work and in the streets was always the progress of the war. We were frequently reminded of the serious side of warfare by the Zeppelin raids, and several bombs were dropped in the vicinity. It was thrilling to see the raiders pinpointed by the searchlights and the skill of the pilots endeavouring to shoot them down.

After several weeks of this, I decided to enlist. I was still two years too young, but like many youths of that era, had no hesitation in telling the recruiting officer that I was 19 years old. I was duly accepted and after being sworn in was posted to the Royal Field Artillery at Woolwich. My stay at the local barracks lasted only two days, for I was then posted to the Royal Garrison Artillery at Great Yarmouth. After a fortnight at the barracks in this town, I was posted, with others, to the Fort of Languard. This was situated on the Suffolk side of Harwich Harbour, which at that period was the anchorage of many fast destroyers and submarines, and was also a flying boat base.

Life at the fort was interesting and I enjoyed working on the guns. Unfortunately, we only fired the guns at the enemy on one occasion. Enemy ships were a little scared of the wily destroyers. It was exciting to see them come in to dock after a foray in the North Sea – they didn't always return unscathed. On one occasion, several were so badly holed that they had to run aground outside the harbour. We had the task of removing quite a lot of ammunition from the magazine of one. I soon began to tire of this almost peaceful existence and, like the rest of the 'boys', volunteered for everything that came along, especially if it meant getting near the front. Within a short time I was on a draft for

Mesopotamia, but didn't get away because I was taken off the draft at the last moment to help train signallers. (I had already become efficient in this type of work when I was a Boy Scout.) I was promoted to the magnificent rank of Supernumerary Lance Bombardier without pay – this rank doesn't exist now. At the end of the course, I was promoted to Corporal with pay. Shortly afterwards I returned to Woolwich to take my riding course and returned six weeks later, a little sore in the rear, happy to have qualified as capable of managing a horse fit for artillery work, but hardly good enough to ride a real charger.

In the early spring, a new battery was formed, and we commenced earnest preparation for the real business of fighting. We trained in pleasant Sussex and Kentish districts and ended our training with a successful gunnery course at Lydd. Then came the final preparations for leaving for France. The battery went to Bristol for equipping and then loading the equipment en route to its final destination – Boulogne. We spent a busy three weeks in Bristol and while there, I met the girl who subsequently became my wife, not that we either imagined this would be the case. I was not at that time very serious about the opposite sex. Of course our short friendship ended with the usual promises to write to each other, which we did, and I certainly am glad about that.

We left Bristol at midnight – I never could understand why troops must be moved at such unearthly hours. We travelled through the night to Folkestone, where we duly arrived early next day. After a hasty but very much enjoyed breakfast of bread and cheese, washed down with a bowl of tea, we were assembled and marched to the docks. We were cheered on our way by many older men, who repeatedly said, 'Wish I was younger.' What a lot of nonsense; I guess they were glad they were too old.

On our arrival at Boulogne, we were marched to the camp, St Martin's Plain, at the top of a steep hill. I was promptly posted NCO i/c Guard. It was just as well, because as always at that period I was without even a sou. To my surprise, I was relieved from guard duties early in the morning, and after a hurried breakfast, we were on our way to the docks and were soon unloading our equipment from the ship and reloading it on the train. By lunchtime we were on our way towards the front; all of us were very hungry but there seemed no hope of having our pangs appeased. Fortunately, our train was the usual freight-carrying train that seemed to stop at every pretext. Perhaps it is as well that it did, because during one of these many stops we were served with chunks of bread and cheese – alas, no tea!

After one day and night of this nightmare journey, we stopped at some outlandish place and for the next few hours were engaged in unloading our gear. We had some more food, but still no tea. Late in the afternoon, the whole column moved off behind a guide. Gunfire could be heard in the distance, but not any sound of small-arm fire, so we assumed that we were many miles from the actual front. Two hours after our start, we halted and were served with tinned stew; as there was no means of heating it, we had to make the most of the conglomeration of meat and potatoes. In spite of the appearance of this food, it tasted very good. Up came the tea at last, but we had hardly recovered from almost a scalded tummy when the order came to 'get moving'. Soon after resuming the journey, we sighted the odd wounded man walking towards us, and then small-arm fire could be heard. Heavy guns were barking defiance from concealed sites by the roadside. It was now dark, and the various coloured lights from Verey pistols were making the sky quite pretty and the frequent flashes from guns made us aware of the closeness of the fighting. At midnight we arrived at our rendezvous. It was thrilling to be greeted by colleagues who had left us ten days ahead in order to prepare the site.

We were soon acquainted with the situation and instructed to rest until daybreak. It was the longest night I have ever endured. Sleep was out of the question because of the noise – a noise which I was soon to become accustomed to. I was so scared that I couldn't pluck up enough energy to take off my equipment. I merely huddled up by the bole of a tree and simply stared into the sky. Daylight was a welcome sight. I discovered we had spent the night in an orchard, which was already minus trees here and there – the stumps of these trees were still there, looking for all the world like grotesque statues. After eating a messy breakfast, cooked by men who, until then, had never even boiled water, we commenced to unload the stores. Later in the afternoon, in my capacity as a signaller, I was instructed to join a party proceeding to the forward area for reconnaissance. We were away until midday the following day. On our return to the battery site we had the misfortune to be heavily machine-gunned, and as a result our commanding officer was killed and our signal sergeant – Johnny Gawthorpe – was badly wounded, and Smithy, who was discovered later to be only 15 years of age, was badly shocked and was returned to England.

On our return to the battery we were besieged with questions from our colleagues as to what kind of conditions we had found. The loss of Major Robinson was a terrific blow to the boys. He was a great guy. The bloody battles of the Somme were now beginning to take heavy toll on our numbers. The slaughter was terrible, men – German and British – were being killed in their hundreds. As a signaller, I was frequently in the vicinity of the front line and on many occasions in no man's land, the name given to the stretch of land between the opposing front lines. Sometimes the trenches were 500 yards apart, but often they were merely 100 yards. It was my task to keep our lines of communication open, in order to transmit messages from the observation post to the guns. It was exciting to observe our shells falling on chosen targets.

Just after Christmas 1917, the brigade command decided to place two howitzers in a forward position in an endeavour to destroy an important concentration point just behind the German lines. It was a very dangerous mission, so volunteers were called for. Having qualified as a gun layer and being at that time much more venturesome, I volunteered, and together with six others, we were detailed to prepare the chosen site for the arrival of the howitzers.

Everything had to be done after dark because the site was under observation from the enemy. We prepared the site and for the remaining hours waiting for the howitzers to arrive, we decided to use an old French dugout. These dugouts were merely holes in the ground, covered with semicircular sheets of corrugated iron, which were supported by a bulk of timber, which in turn was supported by upright bulks. These shelters were sufficient to protect anyone from shell splinters from near bursts, but were no protection against a direct hit. Having found cover, we proceeded to eat our bread and cheese and brew a pot of tea. After this repast, we chatted until, one by one, we dropped off to sleep.

Some little time later, I was awakened by a terrific rush of air and on fully awaking, I discovered that the shelter had been destroyed by a direct hit, but fortunately the shell was a dud and had not exploded. Our immediate task was to get free from the debris, but this was impossible because the supports had collapsed and we were practically sealed in. Fortunately, we were able to breath and, apart from one of our number, appeared to be uninjured. The injured man had been pinned to the ground by a support. We were unable to assist him because we had no means of escaping from the trap, as our only implements were jacknives. He eventually died of shock from the crushing weight of the timber. We shouted for what seemed hours, but no help was forthcoming. Daylight came after what seemed an eternity, and our continued shouting was heard by a passing pioneer company. They quickly discovered us and released us. I had been fairly confident that we would be saved, but on my release I collapsed – the shock had taken effect at last. We were sent down the line for a rest of about seven days and returned to the battery feeling none the worse for our horrible experience.

We remained on the Somme until the following March, then went to Arras and the tremendous battle for Vimy Ridge and the subsequent battles to hold it, later to Messines and the exploding of seven great mines to dislodge the enemy, then to the bloodiest front of all – Ypres. The battery spent nine months of hell in this area. Our casualties were devastating; reinforcements joining us daily. I hardly knew my colleagues when we were up at the front.

Late in the autumn of 1917, I was withdrawn from the signal detachment and attached to the guns for gun-laying. About two weeks after joining the gun team, and when I was in charge, Jerry dropped a gas shell right on to the muzzle of the gun. It killed four of the crew and the rest were wounded in varying degrees. My wounds appeared to be superficial at first, but within minutes I was one great mass of blisters. On realizing we were the victims of the mustard gas the enemy had just commenced to use, I decided to attend the nearby dressing station for first aid. My intention was to get the wounds dressed and then return to action, but I reckoned without the opinion of the MO. He cut the blisters and smothered me with iodine – I nearly jumped through the tin roof. Instead of returning to the guns, I was ordered away to the main dressing station. After further attention by the doctors, we were placed on trains going to the rear. There were two trains waiting and one of the medical orderlies told me the patients on one would be proceeding to Blighty. I secretly hoped that I was on that train. When the train left the danger area, I fell asleep and didn't wake until late the following day. I discovered the train was in a siding and the occupants were being loaded on to waiting ambulances.

The countryside was typically French, so I knew my dreams of getting to England were not to be fulfilled this time. We were actually at a place called Eu, a small town on the Channel coast of France. There were three hospitals situated on a plain overlooking the sea – the Canadian General, a British hospital and an American hospital. I was conveyed to the latter and discovered it to be staffed by voluntary nurses and doctors from Philadelphia. They treated us with the greatest of care and attention. I spent the next six weeks living in comparative luxury after 20 months of squalor and filth.

All good things come to an end, and eventually I was transferred to a transit camp at Dieppe. We remained here for another five days and then I was sent to the artillery base at Harfleur, near Le Havre. Here we were cramped in bell tents – 20 men to a tent. If you had to get out during the night, it was impossible to get back to your own patch. Reveille was sounded at 5.00 a.m. and we were kept busy until 5.00 p.m., with short breaks for meals, which were very skimpy. After two days of this, I decided it was better to be at the front, and soon found myself at the orderly room requesting to be sent back to my unit. My wish was granted and after four awful days of near starvation and bullying by officers and NCOs, who almost without exception had never heard a shot fired in anger, I was on my way to rejoin my battery.

It was three days later that I found my unit in the Ypres Sector. On my arrival, the sergeant major told me I was next in turn for Blighty leave. The authority might come through any minute, but until it did, I had to join my section at the guns. I was a stranger to this particular spot, but on my arrival discovered we were just below the famous Passchendaele Ridge. It was a terrible site, exposed to the enemy observation, the only protection an old German pillbox with the entrance facing the wrong way. The nearest water point was under enemy fire day and night, so we obtained our water from nearby shell holes. It was filthy stuff, but after boiling became fairly tolerable for tea making. We lost three men on the way up to the guns. The journey was hell – mud, mud and still more mud.

After three terrible days of constant shelling by the enemy, I was pleased to hear the battery runner say my leave pass had at last arrived. I was officially relieved and literally ran the whole three miles to the wagon lines. I was soon taking the necessary bath in the disused brewery and, after a clean issue of clothing, was on my way to Poperinghe, where I was to board the leave train. While waiting for the train to leave, we had the awful experience of being shelled by a long-range gun, but fortunately the train was not hit, and after what appeared to be a lifetime, we were on our way to paradise, or the equivalent – ten days in England.

The days went far too quickly, and I was unable to get to Bristol to see my girlfriend. We had corresponded, but our association at that time was merely friendly.

During the ten days I had been on leave, the British had retaken quite a large area from the enemy, but things had simmered down, and the trench warfare was continuing. The country around Ypres was getting worse every day – there was hardly a square yard that was not covered with water or mud. The roads were constructed of planks nailed on runners, but they were constantly being blown sky-high by shell fire. There was a rumour around that the Germans were going to attempt a breakthrough, or that the British were hoping to do the same. There was great activity in the area and hundreds of guns were being manned. The breakthrough did eventually happen, but it was the Germans.

On a bright March morning in 1918, we were told that we were pulling out because the enemy had broken through and had advanced its forces 20 miles on to the Somme. We were sent with others to strengthen the sector. It was not long after our arrival that we could hear heavy gunfire predicting the attack, which came shortly afterwards with disastrous results. The front at this stage was being held by the Portuguese, and they were not well seasoned troops able to withstand a heavy attack, so they naturally gave way. In the ordinary way, the attack would have been stemmed, but the 'Pork and Beans', as the Portuguese were affectionately known, wore uniforms of a similar colour to that worn by the Germans. As a consequence the support troops, who at the time were fresh and did not know they were supporting Portuguese troops, fired on the retreating soldiers, thinking they were Germans advancing. Unfortunately, the enemy obtained a stronghold before the mistake was discovered. They were, however, held, and within a few months the situation was completely reversed. The American troops were beginning to arrive in their thousands, and they were able to relieve many thousands of soldiers from the

Commonwealth who were at that time assisting the French down south.

By the end of the summer we were recovering lost ground daily, and when the Armistice was signed, we had reached the famous battlefield of Mons. We remained there until after Christmas 1918. During that period of the Armistice, I had returned to England for more leave.

During this leave I went to Bristol and renewed my friendship with my first and only love. Owing to the great significance of this leave, I had taken an extra week, but because of the goodwill feeling all around, I was not punished. At the end of January, the men of the battery who had been volunteers were separated from the others and returned to France to await demob. The remainder of the battery, consisting of 'Derby Men' – men conscripted from 1916 onwards – went on to Germany to be part of the occupation forces.

It was almost May before I was sent home for demob at Croydon. At first it was thrilling to be a civilian once again. I spent part of my demob leave at Bristol with Clarice, and we became engaged. It was the greatest moment of my life!

2

On the Beat

After a delightful month's holiday, I decided it was time to start the business of earning a living. The country was in a terrible state, every other man was out of work. I was able after a great struggle to get work with my old employer, but the wages were too low to enable me to get married, so I decided to try my hand as a steward on a New Zealand shipping company vessel. I soon tired of this; the pay was terrible and – a far greater reason – I was in love at last.

Early in the autumn, I decided to become a policeman. Goodness knows why! I had never been over fond of the 'man in blue', although I had never been in contact with them – my father had been too strict for that sort of thing. I enrolled in the Metropolitan Police Force on 8 September 1919, having satisfied the authorities that my character was beyond reproach.

At that time there were two training schools, the extra one instituted because of the large number of recruits. Training was carried out at Peel House (the authorized training centre) and the Eagle Hut. The Eagle Hut, where I was to undergo my training, had been an old wartime club for the American forces in London. It was a large, commodious place with many rooms for lectures and dormitories for students. It was situated on a plot of land now containing Bush House and other big business houses. Owing to the special urgency to have trained police officers quickly, the authorities decided to dispense with the educational training of those men who they considered were up to scratch. Being one of this number, after seven weeks' training in law I was sworn in as a constable. (Today the training takes from 18 months to two years.)

I was posted to 'R' Division with HQ at Blackheath Road, and after the usual interview with the superintendent, was posted to Woolwich. I was of course well acquainted with the district. Parts of the town were not very salubrious and police duty was difficult to perform. Some of the districts, especially the 'Dusthole', were the haunts of crooks and cut-throats. I was not unduly perturbed by this; I considered nothing could be as bad as the last few years. The first few weeks of police duty were not very onerous, in fact I found them boring.

My marriage took place on the morning of 6 November 1919 at All Saints Church, Herbert Road, Plumstead. It was not the elaborate affair that most girls look forward to. I had not the money and was unable to get leave at such an early time in my career, but I was desperately anxious to get married for fear of losing my girl. Competition was just as great then as now, and Bristol was a long way away. (In spite of the absence of bridesmaids with the attendant finery, our marriage has been one of great loyalty and love.) We managed to obtain a couple of rooms on the outskirts of Woolwich and life was for a time very pleasant. Nothing very exciting happened with regard to police duty.

My first real thrill came when I was posted on night duty. Walking the streets at night is quite an odd experience. Of course I was keen to catch my first burglar, or to do something worthwhile. My first months on night duty did nothing to enhance my reputation – it was quite uneventful.

The first ten months as a constable went by without anything thrilling happening, unless the finding of a dead body floating in the river could be classified as thrilling. When I first saw the body, I had visions of being concerned with a murder trial, but the body turned out to be that of a seaman who had been reported lost overboard some weeks before.

I was back on night duty in September 1920, and about this time we were expecting our first baby. On the evening of the 26th, I was compelled to call upon the midwife before reporting for duty; she came before I left home. The night seemed extraordinarily long and it was with anxious thoughts that I arrived home the following morning. The midwife had long since left. The following night was my 'off night', so instead of going to bed, I busied myself around the house; not for long though, because I had to be away to warn the midwife again. She duly arrived and then began the most terrifying period in my life so far. I was plain scared, because my wife was my absolute life. Fortunately, the midwife gave me plenty to do and I was kept far too busy to allow my thoughts to wander. She was an old but experienced Irishwoman who had brought many babies into the world without the assistance of the doctor. It was late that night when I heard – what appeared to me then – the most exciting yell of a new-born baby. I was outside the door like a shot enquiring if Clarice was OK. I was soon admitted and met for the first time my newly born son, who even at that stage looked really handsome. I went on duty the following night with a certain amount of trepidation, but it was an unusually quiet night, and when I arrived home, I found both Clarice and the baby quite well.

Things went smoothly for the first month and I felt as if I was on top of the world. Our great happiness was, however, short-lived. Donald, the new baby, became very fretful and cried daily and sometimes all through the night. After a month of 'days', I was back on night duty again and came home frequently in the mornings to find Clarice lying completely exhausted on the bed, still fully dressed. The least noise would waken the baby and the crying would start all over again. This state of affairs continued for weeks, in spite of the fact that I had consulted the doctor. He had the audacity to say it was merely bad temper on the baby's part. I could not believe that this could be the cause of the continual crying, and felt that something more serious was the matter. I was so convinced of this I sought the aid of the police surgeon. He was at first reluctant to interfere with views of another medico, but my urgent appeals encouraged him to see the baby. He was soon convinced that the crying was a result of internal trouble and had Donald removed to hospital at once. The poor little fellow was found to be suffering from a rupture and, after an operation, he was returned to us, but the delay in treatment had seriously impaired his life and he never recovered from it. I am sure, if I had had the money, I would have brought the first doctor to court for absolute negligence.

We had moved to larger rooms at Eltham while the baby was in hospital, and I was back on day duty once again. One afternoon, the baby was very poorly when I left for afternoon duty. I seemed to have a premonition that he was going to die. At about 4.00 p.m. that day, I saw Clarice coming over the common towards my beat and she was crying, so I knew the worst had happened. It was heartbreaking to hear her announce the death of our lovely little Donald. It was by far the biggest tragedy in our lives. Fortunately time is a great healer of broken hearts. The loss of Donald even now, years later, still lies heavy on my heart.

Where we lived there was quite a journey from the police station to which I was attached, so I used to cycle to and from duty. One morning I was freewheeling down a slope by the Garrison Church when I got into a skid on the tramlines. It had been snowing and the ground was covered with slush. I slid about 50 feet and when I picked myself up I was covered with mud. I was more concerned with having become an object of ridicule to the workmen passing by. Then, as now, a laugh at the expense of a copper was always great fun. I was almost convinced that a policeman's life was not for me – it certainly was not very exciting – but I overcame the desire to give it up.

About this time, the business of living was beginning to become very complicated for the masses. Unemployment was on the increase throughout the country. The aftermath of war was at last being felt all over the world. There were large queues at the labour exchanges and the relieving officers were besieged daily by people anxious to obtain some assistance to maintain body and soul. In those days, the 'means test' was the deciding factor regarding assistance for the needy. As a consequence, all personal savings had to be exhausted before relief could be obtained. This led to trouble and arguments, in fact frequently attacks were made on the officials by recalcitrants. Police officers were engaged at these offices to prevent breaches of the peace. Hunger marches were organized from the provinces to London to draw attention to the unemployment and the plight of the workers in various industries. All these processions had to be accompanied by police to prevent disorder; there was, however, little disorder except from the usual sources. We naturally felt sympathetic towards these unfortunates – many of whom had fought by our side in the war.

This desperate phase in our post-war history passed in due course. The commonplace job of preventing crime and disorder continued without any great incident happening to break what, at times, appeared to be a very monotonous job. I was kept occupied with the usual crop of small offences which necessitated the odd arrest, and a few suicides and street accidents for good measure. I was frequently called to settle family disputes between man and wife, and soon learned that discretion was very necessary in these cases. Women curse their husbands frequently, but woe betide anyone interfering with their men.

While on night duty I caught my first burglar – some 15 months after my first appointment as a constable. It was a dirty damp night and I had just commenced my patrol. As I turned down a lane, I saw a movement which gave me a thrill – a thrill I had waited months for. I ran up some steps, towards the house where I had seen a suspicious light, but I must have been observed, because when I reached the spot all was quiet. I flashed my lamp beam on the door of the house and noticed the door had been forced. I immediately came to the conclusion that the miscreant or miscreants, having seen me, were attempting to escape from the rear of the house. I rushed to the rear and at once was confronted by the burglar – yes, there was only one! He struck at me with his jemmy in order to avoid arrest, but I had been well instructed in the art of self-defence in the police training school, so I quickly had him under my control. Once I had restrained him, he made no further attempt to assault me. We, of course, contrary to widespread belief, did not carry handcuffs, but merely relied on peaceful persuasive methods. We carried truncheons but seldom used them, because every use of this implement had to be reported. Criminals in those days were not usually violent, except in rare cases. This particular prisoner was finally dealt with at the London Sessions, and having previous convictions, he was sentenced to three years.

During the same month of 'nights', I was having a cuppa at the rear of a coffee stall by the ferry. Whilst standing in the shadows enjoying the hot liquid, I overheard a conversation between two customers, one of whom was trying to sell the other a suit. Being suspicious, I asked the man to open the case he was carrying. Instead of complying with my request, he dropped his case and ran towards the tunnel entrance (the foot tunnel connecting South and North Woolwich). I could run fairly well in those days, being a mere 10 stone 5, so I quickly caught my quarry. Joe, the proprietor of the stall, had taken charge of the case. My suspect admitted that he had previously stolen the case from the railway station. He came quietly to the police station, where it was discovered he was an out-of-work seaman trying to raise a little cash for a night's lodgings. He got the lodgings free! Being a first offender, he was sentenced by the magistrate to three months, and took his sentence without any complaint.

On resuming my patrol at about 2.30 a.m., I saw a man reeling about the pavement, with blood gushing from a gaping wound in his wrist. I quickly applied a tourniquet – all police officers are trained in first aid; in fact it is a condition for promotion. I called the ambulance and took him at once to the local hospital. The house surgeon asked me to assist with the various instruments – I could not do that nowadays, because the mere sight of blood makes me feel very sick. He was soon patched up and told he could return home. I offered to accompany him, but much to my surprise he preferred to remain in the hospital. His actions were not at first understood, but he later explained that his wrist injury was caused as a result of a fight with his wife, of whom he was scared. The doctor took compassion on him and permitted him to stay the night.

My busy night was not yet over. At 5.30 a.m., when I was having a last look around prior to going off duty at 6.00 a.m., a woman came up to me to say her father had committed suicide; but on arriving at the house, I discovered he had not succeeded in taking his own life. He was lying with his head in the gas oven, but the gas supply had failed through lack of sufficient money in the meter. He was unconscious, so I rushed him into the garden, and after some artificial respiration he responded and quickly recovered. Like all attempted suicide cases, he was detained for observation for a few days in hospital. It was through the usual causes that he had attempted to take his own life – lack of funds. I knew his sons very well, and they told me later that he had repented and was beginning to regain faith in himself. With all these events, I was a little late in arriving home and found my wife very distressed. Like all policemen's wives, she always dreaded the worst.

Nothing very exciting happened for a while, until one night when I was on 5.00 p.m. to 1.00 a.m. point duty. Nearby was the Oak public house, and being Saturday night, it was filled with thirsty customers. Just about 5.00 p.m., I heard the smashing of glasses and much commotion coming from the public bar. Soon after, the potman came out and called me to prevent further disorder. Police must never enter licensed premises – only in the course of duty. On entering the bar, I found the customers completely cowed by one man, the notorious bully known to local police as 'Bruiser' Brown. He was a man of violent temper who had seriously injured many a police officer with his onslaughts. Of course, though I put on a bold front, I was scared that it would not be long before I was a victim of his violence. To my surprise, when I spoke to him he calmly walked out of the pub and went on his way without uttering a single word to me. Everyone present was dumbfounded at his strange behaviour, and no one was more surprised than I. Some days later the mystery was cleared up. I was visiting my mother, a Christian woman, who was managing a hostel for the down-and-outs. It was a local church effort to provide some sort of comfort to the residents of a squalid section of the community. While there, I saw Bruiser and asked him why he had forgotten his usual arrogance on the Saturday night. He replied, 'Your mother has frequently helped my wife when I have been inside, and when I recognized you, I knew I couldn't harm you.'

Just about this time, we were persuaded to live with a friend at Eltham who had lost her son in the war. She had repeatedly asked us to share her accommodation, so after the death of Donald, we decided to give it a trial. Everything went off well for a time and I used to do odd jobs around the house, such as repairing shoes and reglazing windows. Unfortunately, the loss of her son had somewhat deranged her mind, and now and again she would turn on me and curse me for having come back from the war while her son had died. I eventually got fed up with this conduct and looked for other accommodation. We were lucky, because just about then, my old foreman of the printing days, who also came from my home town, had recently bought a large house in Plumstead and wanted me to have half of it. We naturally took up the offer and moved. We were at last able to get more things for our home and life became much more tolerable.

Some months later, I was back doing point duty outside the Oak. At another pub, the Shakespeare, not far away, a disturbance had started. Apparently, a prostitute and her man friend were having an altercation with a soldier, and as a result a fight ensued. A colleague of mine – Charlie Crawford – was on duty nearby and he was called to quell the disturbance. The miscreants set upon him, but he managed to blow his whistle for assistance. I was quickly on the scene, and together with other officers, we soon had arrested several people mixed up in the general melee.

One or two of the original arrests concerned young soldiers. There were a large number of reservists in the town – men called up for special duties. They were already disgruntled at being recalled, and in addition they were dissatisfied with the attitude of the 'redcaps'. They were ripe for disorder and as a consequence when they heard of the arrest of the soldiers, they decided to attempt to rescue them from their temporary incarceration at the local police station. They besieged the station and attacked the police with bottles and other implements. They even threw these objects from passing buses and in some cases set fire to shop blinds. After order had been restored, we had over 40 soldiers in custody. While the fight lasted it was very hectic, but I must admit I enjoyed every minute of it. For the next month the arrests were patrolled by the army and things became normal once again. A few weeks later the IRA, a gang of young toughs claiming to be members of this illegal organization, began to terrorize the neighbourhood by committing arson. As a means of combating this latest outrage, officers were posted day and night to protect important places – power stations, post offices, etc.

One night, I was on this special duty guarding the local powerhouse at Globe Lane, which stood on the riverside. The tide had just started to ebb and at this spot the depth of the river was about 20 feet close inshore. The Thames ebbs pretty fast. At about 10.00 a.m., five tough-looking customers, subsequently found to have no connection with the IRA, merely bent on having a little sport at the expense of the police, started to rough me up. I put up a show with the aid of my truncheon, but quickly knew that my cause was hopeless without assistance. I could already see my body floating down the river. I was never much of a swimmer, so I was certainly no match for the fast-flowing river. When I thought my resistance was hopeless, I saw a man come from the shadows and he set about the thugs; before I had fully regained my breath, we had subdued three of them and were on our way to the station with them in custody. I was pleasantly surprised to find my rescuer was none other than Johnny Dunbar, a young local fellow who had caused me some trouble one night many weeks before. I had at that time arrested him for assaulting me and when he appeared before the magistrate, the beak asked me if I knew anything about him. I replied 'Nothing, Your Worship, but I understand from my colleagues that he seldom gives police any trouble except when in drink.' The fact that I had spoken in his favour had so impressed Johnny that he was prepared to risk his neck to assist me. Johnny was rewarded by the boys at the station with a silver watch.

Some years after the birth of Don, on 6 June, our Steve was born at Woolwich Hospital for Babies. We had decided to take no more chances with doctors and midwives. It was a quick job for which I was very grateful. I walked with Clarice to the hospital – she insisted that there was no need for a taxi. When we arrived, visiting time for the husbands was in full swing. After I had wished Clarice good luck, I asked the matron if I could ring later to hear how things were going. To my surprise, she replied, 'If you care to hang around for half an hour, I will probably be able to give you all the information then.' While waiting, I had to put up with the hostile stares from the poor husbands who had been temporarily turned out of the ward while Clarice was being admitted. They were soon allowed in again and exactly half an hour from the time I had wished Clarice good luck, I was informed that we had a daughter. It was the next day before I saw my daughter for the first time, and it was a very happy moment for me. Naming our daughter did not give us any trouble because we had already decided, if it was a girl, to name her Stephanie. I always liked nicknames, and thus we were able to call her Steve. It was a popular choice of everyone. She is hardly ever called Stephanie, except on official documents and during special occasions. To us she will always be Steve.

While Clarice was in the hospital, I visited my brother and

his wife on my next day off. They gave me some beautiful flowers to take to Clarice. On the next visiting day, I proudly took these flowers to the hospital, but have never dared carry flowers since. I must have looked a real chump, because all the women in the ward burst out laughing – I suppose I was a clumsy lout at that time.

Steve soon filled the great gap in our lives caused by the death of Donald. She was all I hoped she would be; not too good – who wants a child to be absolutely perfect? She was always cheerful and friendly to all. I never realized this quite so much until years later when she left the family circle for Vancouver. After she had left these shores, people whom I never knew stopped me and enquired how Steve was getting on. We used to romp in the fields, play ball in the park, build snowmen in the garden. In fact, when I was off duty, we were always together. I used to take her to the station, where she was admired by all. She was always taken from us at the annual Christmas party by our many friends, who simply loved to hear her chatter. She enlivened our lives so much that even today we look upon her birth anniversary as our lucky day.

One day, when she was about six months old, I was entrusted to take care of her while Clarice was out visiting. She was sleeping in a small basket-type cradle placed on the sofa. Someone called me while she was sleeping. I had hardly been away a few seconds, when I heard a small whimper. I hurried in and found the cradle upset and Steve lying on the rug. She was not crying, even though she had knocked her head and had the beginning of two lovely black eyes. I was scared, but need not have been, because within days she was quite OK, and her face was unblemished. Another time we were visiting friends when she fell over the rockery and struck her head on a sharp piece of rock. This penetrated her forehead immediately above the eye. The wound bled profusely and in a short time it looked ghastly. Clarice was hysterical with fright, but after washing the wound, I found it to be nothing very serious. Steve, as usual, was quite unperturbed about it.

Life for me in the police force continued with nothing exciting happening very often. The authorities decided to switch the men around a bit, and single men residing in Plumstead were transferred to Woolwich, so that they could occupy the single men's dormitories, while married men, living on Plumstead ground, were to take their place. I lived at Plumstead, so was one of the officers on the transfer list. I was sorry about this because I had become attached to Woolwich, and besides there was far more scope for duty at the principal station. I was on night duty for the last month at Woolwich.

It was November, with the usual fog and general dampness that prevails at this time of the year. My beat necessitated me patrolling down by the quarry after leaving the inhabited part of the beat, and to do this I had to pass down a narrow lane, skirted by fields with an overhanging hedge. While I was walking down this lane on a very foggy night, a strange thing happened to me. I was making my way down the lane, more by instinct than by sight, when I suddenly came up against something soft and wet. I was plainly scared for a minute or two. I put my hand out to feel what it was, and after a time discovered it was the head of a cow who had stretched out her head to obtain some juicy morsel from an overhanging bough. I quickly recovered from the shock and continued down the lane, into the residential part of my beat. I was soon on the edge of my beat, which at this spot skirted the river. Just offshore, large barges – or lighters, as they are commonly known – were lying at anchor or resting on the mud when the tide receded. They were mostly loaded with sugar discharged from nearby vessels. As I approached the river bank, I heard whispered conversation between two men. It being 3.00 a.m., I stopped to hear the conversation, guessing that it might prove interesting. I discovered that these men had stolen two bags of sugar from a barge and were now discussing how they were going to dispose of their spoil. They decided to borrow a truck and sell it to a fence. One of the men said, 'If we see a copper, we'll tell him we are taking it to the station, having found it lying around.' I kept in the shadows until they returned with the truck and then followed them to the main road, and when they walked under a street lamp, I recognized them as two local thieves. Knowing that one of my colleagues would be along soon, I decided to question them, and by the time my colleague had arrived, I had already told them I was going to arrest them for stealing the sugar. This was my last job at Woolwich.

On the following Monday, I commenced duty at Plumstead. Plumstead was heavily populated, but was surrounded by large stretches of undeveloped land, and as a consequence the outlying beats were very uninteresting and didn't afford much scope for police work. One such beat ran the whole length of the Sewer Road – the sewer one side and the walls of the Arsenal on the other. This stretch of the Arsenal contained salvage sheds where valuable metals were reclaimed from munitions and their containers. Whilst patrolling this beat one night, I was surprised to have a heavy bag of copper screws drop at my feet; they had evidently been thrown from the other side of the Arsenal wall. I guessed that arrangements had already been made for an accomplice to pick up the bag, so I hid in the undergrowth, and shortly my patience was rewarded by the appearance of a man who went directly to the spot where the screws were. I immediately arrested him, and some days later, his colleague on the other side of the wall was also arrested.

While playing football a few days later, I twisted my knee. After a lot of trouble with this knee, I had to attend the chief surgeon and he discovered that I had torn the cartilage and ordered an operation to remove the trouble. I was in St Thomas's Hospital for about two weeks. On the day after my discharge from hospital, Clarice's relatives visited us from Swansea and asked me to accompany them to the Wembley Exhibition. My knee resembled a large pudding, but I did not want to disappoint them, so we all went to Wembley and managed to see most of the exhibits. My knee looked very bad, but otherwise showed no ill effects from this expedition.

I was always hoping to become a detective, and made applications by the dozen to become a member of this illustrious branch of the police force. I did not meet with a great deal of success and came to the conclusion that it was a case of 'whom you knew, and not what you knew'. This did not stop me from trying. For the next few years I was constantly applying to be considered for transfer to Fingerprints, Criminal Records etc., but I never appeared to have any success with my efforts. I came to the conclusion that this was merely bad luck, until one day, on the advice of a friend who thought I had the necessary qualifications, I applied for duty with the Special Branch. Still no response to my application. On telling my friend that I had again been unsuccessful, he asked me why I had been turned down. I told him that I did not know. He replied, 'Of course you must know – what did the minute say?' It was then I discovered that all applications were duly acknowledged and the applicant informed as to why he had not been accepted. I had never heard any more after applying, so I suspected that my applications had never been forwarded to the right channels, and discovered that whenever I had applied, a certain inspector had always been on duty. We had never got on very well together because I had earlier accused him of favouritism. I told him that I suspected he had destroyed my applications. He denied this accusation, but when he made no move to place me on report for making such an accusation, I knew he was telling lies. After that episode I was more determined than ever to get out of uniform. Clarice was tired of my efforts, but at the same time she was disappointed.

Life at Plumstead was not very exciting. One night I found several horses straying on the road, so I mounted one and drove the rest to the pound. The pound is a local reception centre for animals that have strayed from homes and fields. They are of course returned to their rightful owners on the payment of a small fee, plus a fine if they had strayed as a result of carelessness on the part of the owner. Quite often gates of fields were left open by thoughtless courting couples and children.

One night I caught a burglar, but in a most unorthodox manner. A friend of mine used to park his car at the back of his premises – usually unlocked – so that I could sit in it to partake of my supper whilst on the beat. I always carried a small spirit stove to warm up my tea and we were allowed half an hour to take our refreshments, so the use of the car was very welcome. I had finished my repast and was about to take a puff at my pipe when I saw a figure approaching the rear of the shops. I jumped quickly out of the car and arrested the miscreant just as he was forcing the lock of a door with a jemmy. He looked very surprised when I grabbed him and he merely said, 'It's a fair cop, Guv!' This was his second break-in that night; it was subsequently discovered that he had entered other premises further up the road. In the first break-in he had placed some sticky paper over the window and then smashed the glass – the sticky paper prevented the noise of broken glass. He had then opened the door by placing his hand through the hole and opened the latch from the inside.

On 14 August, our second son was born at the same hospital as Steve. Where Steve's birth had been a great joy, Arthur's arrival was tragic. Not because he was unwanted – we desired a son in the family – but because tragedy had once again beset us. Every mother and father loves to have a boy around the house; a son and daughter are a great blessing. On my arrival at the hospital soon after his birth, I found Clarice stricken with grief; in fact it was months before she recovered her normal placid outlook on life. I was at a loss to understand her condition, until I was ushered into the matron's room and she told me that Arthur had a hare lip and a cleft palate. It seemed terrible that such a thing should happen to us. The hospital people were very good and within a few weeks Arthur was admitted to Charing Cross hospital and shortly afterwards he was operated on by Mr Luke, the surgeon. At that early age, only the lip could be done, but we were assured that Mr Luke was known all over the world for his skill with such matters.

Arthur's outward appearance was greatly improved, but the real trouble was only beginning. The operation to remedy the cleft palate was not possible until Arthur was three or four years old. He had this operation later and a small piece of his posterior was grafted in the roof of his mouth. He was unable to suckle and every morsel of food had to be spoonfed to him. It was an agonizing procedure. It took ages to feed him, and he suffered terribly from wind. By the time the poor child had been relieved of that irritating condition, it was time for another feed. This state of affairs lasted almost 18 months and by that time we were completely exhausted. Our very limited savings were gone and we were, to put it mildly, financially embarrassed. I had to sell my modest insurance policies to save us from getting into debt.

If this was not enough, Arthur, who was never strong, owing to the weakness of his chest caused by the cleft palate, developed congestion of the lungs. He became very ill and needed watching day and night. A nurse came during the day and I watched over him at night. My chief inspector had arranged my duties to enable me to do this. Arthur could eat nothing and the only sustenance he had was a small tablet, taken three times a day, and the occasional tiny dose of whisky. This of course was administered on doctor's orders.

He had been ill for three weeks when the doctor told me, 'I'm afraid he will not last the night – if there is any change, let me know at once!' I watched Arthur closely through the night, except that at about 3.30 a.m. I dozed off, but quickly awoke when I heard the patient making a strange noise. I was very sleepy, but alert enough to give him a little whisky. In my haste, I gave him almost a spoonful of the spirit instead of the three drops. He almost choked and then appeared to renew his breathing much more rapidly than before; colour came to his pallid face. I rubbed his chest and decided to stay by him and not bother the doctor.

The doctor arrived earlier than usual on the following morning. He expressed great pleasure at Arthur's appearance. I told the doctor what I had done and he laughingly said, 'Though I don't advise the treatment on any future occasion, it certainly did the trick this time.'

Arthur continued to make progress and just a week before Steve's birthday anniversary, I applied to be allowed to sit for another examination for entrance to Special Branch.

I was duly called up for the examination and interview, both of which I passed, and was told that I would be transferred to Special Branch on the following Monday – Steve's birthday. Out of the four who had passed the examination, I was the only one who had not had the benefit of a public school education. The Assistant Commissioner (as he was known then) was on the point of turning me down, but the superintendent in charge of Special Branch said, 'This man has special qualifications which more than offset the lack of public schooling.' His remarks impressed the Assistant Commissioner and I was duly accepted.

Before writing of my experiences in the branch, I must briefly recall some of the memorable days I spent in uniform. On special occasions, we were paraded in our best tunics, bedecked with medals, and our boots and buttons shining. We then entrained for London, where we lined the streets when important events took place. The public always seemed so friendly on these occasions and I felt elated at being a member of the section chosen to line the route. We got to close quarters with occupants of the carriages conveying important people to weddings and funerals.

I was present on such occasions as the burial of the Unknown Warrior, the funerals of Queen Alexandra and Earl Haig, the weddings of the Duke and Duchess of York and the Duke of Kent and Princess Marina, and the visits of foreign notabilities. On a couple of occasions I was on special duty at Epsom Racecourse on Derby Day, and also at Ascot.

3

Special Branch

On 6 June 1927, I reported for duty with the Special Branch. The Branch was formed in 1883 to combat the Fenian outrages of that period. After being briefed as to my future duties and being introduced to some of my new colleagues, I was given the rest of the day to hand in my uniform. I found Special Branch occupying two floors of St Stephen's House with a back entrance through Cannon Row Police Station yard. The Special Branch is a section of the Criminal Investigation Department, concerned mainly with crime connected with the state. The Branch is also responsible for the safety of the Royal Family, visiting heads of state and government members. One of the many duties we were called upon to perform was the protection of our Royal Family. On occasions the King – George V – used to ride in Rotten Row early in the morning and it was always the duty of a member of Special Branch to position himself in the vicinity to prevent any untoward incident. I know of no such incident ever occurring.

Members of the Branch are posted to various ports to assist in controlling the entry of undesirable aliens and the arrest of persons endeavouring to escape after having committed crimes, also checking arrivals and departures of international criminals. The Branch is also responsible for enquiring as to the antecedents of applicants for British Naturalization. This latter work affords some very interesting enquiry work, which calls for ingenuity and tact.

and is far more technical than ordinary criminal work. We also had the very important job of keeping up to date with the movements of international suspects – they abound in every country and their main aim in life seems to be the overthrow of one system of rule for that of another – and suspects who attempted to sell the secrets of one country to another. I took a large part in all these phases of detection work. When I commenced my duties at the Yard, I had only a vague idea of what I would be called upon to do.

Clarice was looking forward to the new job because she was thinking in terms of less night duty – she had never been happy when I was on night duty.

I entered the Branch at the season of the year when the Royal Family attend many social functions and theatres. During these visits, members of the Branch had to patrol the routes and the vicinities of the places of call, in an inconspicuous way, of course. As a consequence I was engaged on duty until the early hours of the morning, for many weeks. Though I was keen about the new job, knowing that duties would become more congenial with experience, Clarice was getting a little disturbed. I think she thought I was gadding about town, and it was difficult to explain to her because some of the jobs that kept me out late were of a secret nature. She became reconciled to things as time went on.

I found my colleagues in the Branch to be rather better educated than the average police officer. They were very helpful and I soon adjusted my life and settled down to make a success of my duties. Most of the members of the Branch were linguists and a few were qualified as shorthand writers. I was a shorthand writer with a very good speed. In addition to our ordinary duties, on first joining the CID, all members have to pass the examination in Criminal Jurisprudence. We had to attend classes every day for six weeks and then sat for the examination. Failure meant a return to uniform duty with no second chance. Fortunately I liked the classes and was not surprised to find my name amongst the first six passes. This examination also constituted the first exam for promotion. Promotion, I discovered, was a slow business in the Branch and it was to be six years before I was able to call myself Detective Sergeant. Before that time elapsed, I had many and varied experiences, including a spell away from the Yard on detached duty. More about that later.

It was not long before I had put my shorthand abilities to the test. Taking notes at meetings is quite an experience and calls for lots of patience and an even temper. Sometimes admittance to meetings was difficult to obtain, owing to the nature of the discussion, so all sorts of subterfuges had to be employed to gain access. Sometimes notes had to be taken while lying on my stomach with my ear glued to a ventilator. It must be realized that some of the meetings about which we had to obtain information were gatherings of political intriguers. Information of illegal action is not sufficient; more concrete evidence must be obtained, such as a report containing the actual words spoken. At some meetings similar to those I attended, Communist and Fascist utterances were of such a nature that if the listeners had taken immediate action on the advice of the speakers, dangerous situations would have arisen. We always had to take into account the temper of the public at that particular moment. Fortunately, there were always humorists amongst the audience and they were often able to ease the tension. Information gathered from meetings was often very useful – agitators previously unknown were able to be identified and noted for future reference. Free speech is highly regarded by the British and the letting off of steam is very beneficial.

Though, as a shorthand writer, I had to attend many meetings, my other duties were just as onerous on occasions. I was frequently called upon to make numerous enquiries with very little information to start with. As Special Branch officers dealing with matters affecting the state, we had to make our enquiries as unostentatiously as possible. It was often most important to prevent the person or persons being investigated from knowing that the police were interested in their activities. Though their conduct at times constituted a danger to public well-being, they were far from being guilty of any crime. I obtained much valuable information during the course of my enquiries and, as far as I know, I was able to keep my identity as a police officer secret. I used various methods of approach – sometimes I would assume the role of a milkman endeavouring to obtain new customers, or a commercial traveller, a school inspector or even an insurance investigator. The latter ruse enabled me to obtain very important information on many occasions. My successes were due because this particular role enabled me to be invited into houses. I was able to tell a 'tall story' which often appeared to be very convincing, judging the results of the enquiry. It was essential to have a receptive mind because more often than not the information had to be memorized, as it was impossible to commit it to paper.

For a period I was engaged with other officers collating information regarding the activities of Indian students who were supporters of the Indian Congress Movement. While engaged on this work, I came into contact – not socially – with prominent Indian Nationalists such as Nehru, Krishna Menon and Gandhi. On occasions well-known political agitators would suddenly disappear from public activities. In some cases they had chosen to retire from the political arena, but others adopted this method to work in the background. They, unfortunately for themselves, did not understand the tenacity of the Branch. With our carefully compiled dossiers, it was often possible in a very short time to state their exact whereabouts. The forgers of travel documents were frequently the subject of enquiry.

One important duty I was called upon to perform was the investigation of potential applicants for British citizenship. Many excellent people have become naturalized British subjects, but it sometimes happens that undesirables endeavour to become citizens. As a result, all these enquiries have to be performed with the utmost zeal; even so, the final decision rests entirely with the Home Office. Sometimes an adverse report by an investigator is ignored. Such a case with which I was connected was ignored, in spite of my report. I thought this particular person, a German, was intending to use his British citizenship as a means of obtaining access to places he would not have been able to enter as a German. In spite of the adverse report I submitted, he was granted citizenship. I need not have worried, though, because the authorities were well aware of what they were doing. When the war with the Nazis was imminent, the most dangerous members of that community were rounded up just prior to the outbreak of hostilities, and this erstwhile German citizen was one of those arrested.

Just as I was reporting off duty one evening, I was instructed to proceed to Gravesend to board a new Soviet vessel which was due to arrive at London. This vessel was built entirely by Russian labour and in a Russian shipyard. Her maiden voyage was being celebrated by conveying citizens of the Soviet Union to England as the guests of the British Cooperative Society at Leicester. The passengers were reputed to be workers who had performed excellent service in the first Five Year Plan. My duties were to obtain what information I could regarding the itinerary of the visit. I obtained the assistance of the Immigration Inspector and boarded the vessel with his officers, as an assistant. It was a strange but interesting experience. We boarded the Gravesend reach and remained there until the early hours of the next morning. I assisted a Russian-speaking immigration officer at his interrogations – acting as a clerk. We were treated very courteously and were invited during the course of the evening to a meal of Russian food. I partook of some delicious caviar and liked it, and we were served with vodka – a very potent concoction. Before retiring in a spacious bunk, I listened for a while to an impromptu concert by the crew, in which balalaikas predominated. One of the performers I discovered to be an erstwhile American citizen, one of the many recruited experts. He proved not only to be an excellent musician but an equally good informant. In some strange way, our thoughts were expressed to each other and I obtained some useful data from him. It was, of course, not known at that time if his information was genuine, but I was elated to be informed later that the 'stuff' I had collected was true in every detail.

After having been in the Branch for just over two years, I was seconded for duty at Gravesend. Special Branch perform duty at principal ports in England and at that period officers were also stationed at Rotterdam and Paris. Gravesend is an important post insofar as ships leave and arrive from all parts of the world and numerous small vessels make daily runs to and from the Continent. I was pleased to have been chosen for this particular duty because I love the sea and everything connected with it and also because my duties would give scope for covering all types of detective work. There was also an additional attraction – port duty meant an extra allowance for detached duty and by jingo we still needed the money. A further benefit to be obtained was the possibility of renting a house. Since our marriage we had had our name down for a council house, but getting a house under this scheme seemed hopeless. We were tired of the flat we occupied at Plumstead – it was far too noisy there and certainly not very congenial for the children. With these thoughts most prominent in my mind, I reported for duty at Gravesend on the following Monday.

I was greeted by the officer in charge, Harold Keble; as was customary in the Branch, we always used Christian names, so henceforth he was known to me as Harold. The colleagues he introduced me to were Sid Barnes (never known to smile, so nicknamed 'Smiler'), Bill Hastings, a jovial and generous individual, and lastly Joe D'Mora, a carefree older man of Spanish extraction. I obtained lodgings with a widow, Mrs Brown, and discovered that she had five other boarders, all members of the Waterguard, and excellent fellows they were. I became very attached to one of their number, Ernie Thomas. I remained in digs with Mrs Brown for about five weeks. By that time I had managed to obtain the tenancy of a new house, which I leased for the next three years. I was ably assisted in this matter by Bill. He was a great guy, always willing to help with everything. It was a tremendous thrill when the family arrived and we moved into the new house. With the extra money I was receiving for detached duty, we soon furnished every room and also became the proud possessors of a piano. Steve attended music lessons and life in general was really great. We were on top of the world and no family could have been happier. Life was one great adventure in which all the family could participate.

I found my duties consisted of boarding all types of vessels, both from the Continent and faraway places. We boarded them mostly as they were proceeding upriver, either from the Customs launch, the pilot cutter, tugs, or from small boats manned by watermen. It was thrilling climbing a 'Jacob's ladder' for the first time. I became quite an expert at this. On one occasion I was boarding a liner travelling up the river by this means, when the ladder slipped – it had not been fastened properly to the rails. Fortunately, I managed to hang on and the bosun aboard managed to grab the ladder as it slipped off. Apart from getting my feet wet and breaking a finger, I was none the worse for my experience. It was certainly a good job that the bosun had seen my plight, because I was the last one to board the ladder, and the launch that had taken us to the ship had already cast off.

Our main duties were to keep our eyes open for wanted criminals, either entering or leaving the country, and anything else that might be of interest to the police authorities. We worked in close cooperation with the Immigration and Customs officers. I found the latter far more pleasant to work with, and in addition to the information they were able to impart to us, we were often able to give them information regarding smuggling. We always worked in close harmony to our mutual gain.

The smaller vessels were always suspect because of the ease with which they could manoeuvre in shallow water. They often brought in people trying to land illegally and frequently engaged in smuggled goods. The larger liners of the Shaw Saville Line, Orient Line and the Peninsular & Orient Line left and arrived at scheduled periods. On their arrival they were first boarded by the port doctor, who sometimes conveyed us to the various ships, but of course we were not allowed on board until he had issued his clearance certificate. We had to attend all these vessels when they arrived and when they embarked passengers. We studied the ship's manifests and then looked around the vessel for suspicious characters. In the dock precincts we were often ably assisted by the Port of London detectives, who knew every inch of the vessels, and what was more important, they had contacts who were often of great assistance.

Apart from our interest in the passengers, we also watched the signing on of crews. On occasions it is possible for members to be signed on at the last moment and this is obviously a good way of getting out of the country without attracting too much attention.

Whilst watching bona fide passengers, there was an additional duty of keeping an eye on the sharks who prey on emigrants during the journey to and from the docks. These people board the trains from London and get into conversation with travellers, pretending they are leaving on the same vessel. It is surprising how gullible some passengers are. They give away intimate information and these sharks are quick to cash in. They pass off dud cheques and obtain money from the passengers. They even impersonate ship's officials. It is customary for a purser to advise passengers to deposit their valuables with him at his office. Often one of these thieves will call at cabins, purporting to be a ship's official – even wearing a peaked cap for the purpose – and offer to take care of any valuables. The offer is unfortunately often accepted and it is some hours later when the passenger discovers he has been tricked.

I had the good fortune to catch one of these rats. I was making a tour of the vessel when I chanced to hear a conversation between a suspect and an old lady. She was just about to hand over a considerable amount of jewellery. The old lady had been instructed beforehand to take her valuables to the purser's office and the crook had heard the instructions; he immediately donned an official-looking peaked cap and informed the lady in question that he was a representative from the purser. He had convinced her that it was not necessary for her to go to the office personally, and she was just handing over the valuables when I appeared on the scene. I arrested him and he was subsequently sentenced – not his first conviction by any means.

Sometimes these thieves pretend to be passengers and get unsuspecting people to change dud cheques, on the pretence that they are short of ready cash and have certain bills to pay before the vessel leaves. Sometimes criminals would be travelling with stolen goods in their possession and, knowing they would be picked up at the port of call, in London or elsewhere in England, they would leave the vessel at a French Mediterranean port and arrange for their baggage to be picked up when the vessel arrived in London. Being on friendly terms with most of the baggage masters, we used to obtain information of baggage that was to be called for, and then we would keep a watch on it when it was due to be collected; more often than not, we managed to get the actual criminal by keeping observation on his or her helpers.

We would often get information that certain criminals were expected to arrive. In these cases we would keep observation and, if seen, they would be detained until the London or country officer concerned arrived at the port.

On one occasion I was attending the embarkation of passengers on the *Batavier,* a Dutch vessel plying between London and Rotterdam. This vessel discharged and embarked passengers at Gravesend, but unloaded and reloaded cargo at the Pool of London, quite close to the Tower of London. The passengers travelled to and from London by a special train from Victoria. Some passengers travelled to the embarkation pier by road, but on the way they passed through the controls. One evening I was watching the passengers as they passed through the controls, and later went to the pier head to have a final check before the vessel left. I was leaning on the rails of the pier overlooking the deck of the vessel when I noticed a passenger who I was sure had not passed through the controls (I had a good memory for faces). I called this person ashore and requested him to produce his passport. He made the usual protest, but by that time I was convinced his description fitted that of a man wanted some three weeks before by the Grimsby police. There was of course an element of doubt in my mind because it seemed strange that a wanted man should choose to embark at Gravesend when he could just as easily have embarked at Grimsby. I had to make a decision quickly because the captain wanted to cast off. Under the circumstances and because I trusted my memory, I decided to detain the man. On my arrival at my office, I studied the wanted circulars, and then knew I had not made any mistake, in spite of the terrible threats I was receiving from my suspect. I took him to Gravesend Police Station and had him detained there until the arrival of an officer from Grimsby. He still protested his innocence. On the arrival of an escort from Grimsby, he freely admitted that he was the man wanted. He was curious to know how I had discovered him. He told me that he had arranged a passage to Canada via the Hook of Holland; if he had sailed on a liner from England, he knew he would have been picked up immediately. After the offence was committed, he drove to London and stayed with a friend, and together they planned how he could leave without being detected. His friend discovered that passengers sometimes arrived by road, so they decided to hide for a while and then get away on the *Batavier* by arriving just as she was due to leave. He figured this way everyone would be too busy to notice any late arrivals.

This capture helped me very much with my approaching promotion and I also received a reward and a commendation from the Commissioner of Police. There were several episodes of this nature throughout the four years I spent at Gravesend.

I thoroughly enjoyed the thrill of exploring the large liners, and was frequently invited to marvellous meals on board. On some of the vessels, I took Steve to show her around; how she loved the ice cream on the American boats. It was a wonderful experience to meet so many interesting people arriving and leaving for Australia and New Zealand, North and South America, the Far East, the Mediterranean ports and Russia, Norway and Sweden.

I was invited to take dinner on one of the 'Maru' vessels sailing between London and Japan, so Clarice accompanied me one evening. We had a lovely meal and took a glass of sake with the purser. Clarice wasn't too comfortable during the meal because of the constant attention by the Japanese stewards – she was a shy thing at that time. Frequently, it was my happy task to board vessels from the Dutch East Indies and how interesting it was to discuss matters with people from such places as Bangkok, Sumatra and tea and rubber planters from India and Malaya and even cattle ranchers from the Argentine. In the years at Gravesend, I met and drank with people from all over the world, even from Iceland. Some of the most entertaining folk travelled on small cargo vessels with accommodation for about 12 people. One day I would meet a bunch of teachers from the Pacific coast of America, then homecoming officials from the East.

I found Bill Hastings, one of my colleagues I mentioned earlier, very helpful, and we became firm friends. We frequently worked together and managed to obtain some useful information long before the others because we were friends with some of the tugboat skippers and thus managed to get aboard the vessels as soon as they reached the Thames. I loved the trips on the tugs, especially the feel of the tremendous power from their engines and the ease with which they manoeuvred about. Sometimes we would board a ship from a small launch used by the local agent. There were times when we had to attend vessels in the docks late at night, and the fog would descend rapidly and the river become hidden by a thick blanket. The ferry would stop running, but we often got back to Gravesend in small rowing boats manned by those great river experts, watermen.

These men, born and bred by the river, knew everything there was to know about the currents and other hazards. They were quite uncanny in handling their crafts in the densest fog. They used their acute sense of hearing and could steer a boat under anchor chains as if it was broad daylight, and sometimes we could not see the other occupants of the boat. The ships' sirens would be sounding continuously, and they would guide their craft by listening. It always seemed a miracle to me how they managed, because when the ebb tide is running the current is very strong and in a few seconds the boat could drift many yards.

After I had been at Gravesend about two years, Bill Hastings was recalled and his place was taken by Basil Finch. At this time, I had bought a second-hand motorcycle combination from Harold Keble, and we enjoyed many trips to the seaside and the country. Basil was an engineer before he joined the police, and his knowledge of engines proved very useful. With his assistance, I became interested in radio and built myself a set capable of receiving a worldwide programme. Shortly after this, Harold was recalled to the Yard and replaced by Ernie Tansley. They were merely routine changes to prevent a man from getting rusty. I didn't care too much for Tansley, he was too much of a know-all.

The Dunkirk steamers – plying at that time between Tilbury and Dunkirk – decided to make use of Southend Pier for disembarking passengers in times of fog. Fog is a great nuisance on this stretch of the river. It would come down and remain sometimes for three or four days and no vessel would be able to move, unless it was one of the small vessels whose skippers were just as acute as the watermen. The vessels would drop their 'hooks' when the fog came down, and when it finally lifted, there would be one mass of ships covering the surface of the river. This sometimes constituted a great danger because the vessels swing in a big arc on their anchor chains when the river flows and ebbs.

After three years at Gravesend, I expected the 'return to London' to come through, but instead I was instructed to remain a further year. It meant changing accommodation because I could have the house we occupied only on a three years' lease. I soon found another place, but the garden was full of tall grass, which I had to cut first with a sickle. Not having used one of these tools before, it was not long before I nearly severed a finger from my left hand. I had to go to the hospital to get it stitched, and finished the grass cutting with a pair of shears. We were at that time friendly with Charlie Walker and his family. He had been a policeman on the local force, but after returning from the war decided to start in business on his own account. We had many nice trips together and sometimes I would accompany him on a mission to collect overdue money.

At the end of the fourth year at Gravesend, Steve passed her scholarship examination for entrance to county school. I was afraid if I was recalled to London and we left the county of Kent, she would miss her chance, so we decided to try to get a house on the Kent side of London. I eventually bought one at Welling, and Steve was admitted to Bexleyheath College for Girls.

4

Spies and Subversives

On my return to London, I was instructed to assist Alf Waldron in the protection of Mr Cordell Hull, the Secretary of State of the United States, and also the other members of the mission who were attending a conference in London. It was the International Monetary Conference of 1933. The American and Italian representatives, led by Count Grandi, were in residence at Claridges Hotel and the conference was being held at the Kensington Museum.

I derived much pleasure from accompanying Mr Hull. We often walked the blocks in the evening and frequently engaged in interesting conversation. He was a very quietly spoken man, and appeared to be far removed from the usual bounciness of the average American. I remember asking him one evening how the meeting had gone, he replied, 'I'm sure I can't say – your politicians are so shrewd that I don't know if they mean yes when they say yes. I thought we Americans were astute, but there, I suppose we have not been politicians long enough.' When he left the country some three weeks later, he gave me a lovely silver cigarette case and an autographed photograph of himself.

Among the contingent from the USA were several senators, one a pompous individual, Senator Cox from Georgia. The senator I liked most was Senator Pitman from Nevada. He was a pleasant man but addicted to heavy drinking. His chauffeur, hired from a local firm, was well acquainted with the drinking dives in and around London, and he soon introduced them to the senator. There were several American newspaper men among the party; an outstanding member of this fraternity was Mr Bullitt, who made quite an impression later in Russia. When the time came for the party to leave for home, Mr Pitman was missing. It had never been our task to protect him, but even so, I had to find out what had happened to him. I merely sought out the driver and soon discovered that the erring senator was drinking heavily at a secluded restaurant not too far from Maidenhead. He eventually returned to the States.

While we were at Claridges, we were invited to take our meals at the hotel – free of charge, of course – and what meals they were. Claridges is a top-class hotel and a large number of prominent people stayed there whilst in London. During the three weeks I was there, ex-King Alfonso of Spain was a guest. He stayed there with his charming wife, Princess Beatrice, just after he abdicated from the throne of Spain. Douglas Fairbanks, senior, was also a guest at the hotel. I was always amazed at his agility. He seemed wonderfully fit and on one occasion I saw him jump over his sports car. His constant companion at this time was Lady Ashley. He became one of her many husbands.

After this pleasant interlude from the normal work of Special Branch, I was soon back in the thick of the enquiries and observation rackets. I was attached for a short period to a special squad engaged in recording the activities of a society which was engaged in upsetting the life of the community by committing acts of sabotage. It was our duty to find out all we could about new arrivals in the country. This work entailed many long hours of observation and 'shadowing'. We met at a pub, the rendezvous of these people. All new arrivals were noted for descriptions etc., and when the pub closed, we would each choose a new arrival and then 'house' him.

On one occasion, I was following one of these suspects, who in a latter period proved to be a prominent leader of the society; he subsequently became a great danger and after his arrest he was sentenced to 20 years.

After he left the pub at about 11.00 p.m., he strolled to a coffee stall, where after some conversation with a female, he left with her. I followed them through side streets. At this time of night, following suspects becomes very difficult and all sorts of ruses have to be adopted to prevent the person from knowing he is being followed. They eventually entered a house, and I was secretly hoping that was to be the final phase, but no such luck. He emerged alone and continued his rambling. He seemed uncertain as to what his next move should be.

After a time, he hurried off to the outskirts of north-west London and arrived at a house well known as a haunt of these people. It was now 3.00 a.m. and he let himself in with a key. After satisfying myself that he was bedded down for the night, I decided to make my way home – in this case, the other side of London. It was too late to get a taxi in that district, but I was fortunate enough to get a lift to Piccadilly on a special bus. We were not allowed to ride on these buses normally, but the conductor happened to be an old wartime colleague of mine. It was getting on for 4.00 a.m. when I got off the bus at the Circus and I still had another eight miles to travel home. I managed to get on an all-night tram which took me as far as New Cross and then I started to walk to Plumstead. I had not walked far when a car stopped and the driver asked me the way to Woolwich. I disclosed my identity, and he offered me a lift. He was a young Artillery officer stationed at Woolwich and he kindly drove me right to my house.

It was almost 5.00 a.m. when I crawled into bed. Even so, I was greeted by Clarice with 'You've been drinking.' What a nose that woman used to have. I had had my last drink at 10.30 p.m. It was hardly worthwhile taking the trouble to undress, but I did, and after two hours' sleep, was washed and away to the Yard, where I had to have my report ready by 10.00 a.m. Late nights did not excuse one from this duty. After putting in my report, it became the duty of another officer to make the enquiries to identify the suspect. This system proved very useful in later years.

Two or three days later, I was handed an enquiry by my inspector. I was required to trace a man wanted for passport forgeries. All I had to start with was an old photograph – ten years old – and an address where this person resided about 15 years before. His proper name was not known, but I was given several aliases that he might use. This scanty information was nothing new to us – most of our initial enquiries were like this. A search of records did not help very much, so I set off for the original district. I was not surprised to get negative information for a start. After meditating my next move, I entered a local pub to buy a drink and a piece of bread and cheese. While sitting at the bar enjoying my beer, I noticed a porter enter (most of these districts are served by good-character individuals trying to obtain a living by carrying and taking messages, for which they are licensed by police). I got into conversation with this man, and showed him the old photo. After some hesitation, he recognized the photo to be that of a man residing in the district, but he could not add to this information. I set off for the neighbourhood and kept observation.

I maintained this observation for the next two days, but did not see anyone leave the premises where this man was supposed to be living. However, I noticed two cars parked outside. I took a note of the registration numbers and spent the morning of the following day enquiring at the Registration Office to find out the owners of the cars in question, and was elated to discover that one of the cars was owned by a man whose name was one of the aliases.

I remained on observation, knowing that someone must leave or enter the house at some time. However, I was in the vicinity for several more days before I saw a man talking to someone at the door. It was only a fleeting glimpse, but remarkably like the man in the photo. I was by this time almost sure this was the man the inspector wanted to interrogate, so I decided to make my report. The following day, the inspector and his sergeant, together with another officer and myself, went to the vicinity of the house. I took up observation on the front, and my colleague on the rear of the house. The inspector and his sergeant were admitted to the house. Some two hours had elapsed and I and my colleague on observation were convinced that the interview was already in progress. Just about then, I saw a man leave the house next door and run down the street. Though I only saw his back, I was somehow convinced that he was the man we were after. I consulted my colleague and told him of my suspicions, but both came to the decision that this could not be so because the man was already being interviewed by the inspector. Much to our dismay, half an hour later, the inspector came out and said he was unable to get the man to leave his bedroom for the interview. Naturally, I told him what I had seen, and we went immediately to the house next door, where we were admitted, and quickly discovered the skylight at the top of the stairs was wide open, and on further investigation it was obvious that someone had passed from one house to the other by climbing across the roof, which I must add was not visible from the ground.

We covered the route the escapee had taken and forced our way into his bedroom, and of course after what had happened, we were not surprised to find it empty. Fearing the man might attempt to leave the country, an 'All Ports' message was sent out. I, however, had a hunch that he would return to the house or someone would contact him, so I requested to be allowed to remain in the vicinity.

Some hours later my patience was rewarded. Later in the afternoon, I saw a woman leave the house. I followed her into Hyde Park, but she was obviously aware that she would be under surveillance, so after staying in the park for a short while, she returned to the house. She spoke to no one during this time, but I did notice that she paused for a short while on the outward walk and, after glancing around, continued her journey. After she had returned to the house, I purposely made myself conspicuous to her, in order to delay her next move, then I slipped away to make a little investigation around the spot where she had stopped.

In a back street I discovered one of the cars I had earlier seen outside the house. I made a few enquiries and

Wedding Day

6 November 1919
Myself and Clarice

Myself and Clarice

My Mother Maud and
Father Arthur

Myself and army buddies, World War I, France

Myself and friend

Clarice and myself en route for Norway August 1946

Clarice and myself arriving at Oslo East railway station – 11.15 p.m. August 20, 1916 guests of King Haakon VII at his summer palace

Summer palace of King Haakon VII – Oslo, Norway

Clarice and myself at King Haakon's ski lodge

Clarice at Kongsgaarden, King Haakon's summer palace

Clarice and myself leaving Oslo on our way home after a visit with King Haakon as his guests at the King's summer palace, Kongsgaarden, and being attended by one of the King's personal chauffeurs, Raedar

H.M. King Haakon
of Norway
1905–1957

Myself

Cordell Hull.
Elected to the senate 1930, appointed by President Roosevelt as Secretary of State 1933

Nils and Per aboard the Svanen

discovered the owner of the parked car had entered a small hotel nearby that day. I entered the hotel and was very relieved to find the 'wanted' man sitting in a corner. I informed him as to my identity, although it was obvious he already knew, and detained him until the arrival of the inspector. It subsequently transpired he had been in touch with his wife, the woman I had followed, and had made arrangements for certain things to be given to him in order to make his escape. Her little tour had been a safeguard – she was just as wise to the situation as the police.

My action in the matter pleased my inspector and his final report contained a glowing account of my part in leading to the arrest of the man. I was particularly pleased with the Commissioner's commendation, the wording of which was as follows: 'It was only as a result of this officer's perspicacity that the prisoner was finally brought to justice'. At the end of the week my name appeared in Orders: 'Detective Constable A. Coates is promoted to the rank of Detective Sergeant w.e.f. . .' etc. My promotion was merely routine and solely dependent on my having passed the necessary examination and the Selection Board. Of course the commendation assisted my progress by the Selection Board.

I was then engaged with other officers in obtaining evidence against two men suspected of espionage. My duty was to ascertain the accommodation address being used by the culprits. On this assignment I was assisted by a woman detective – those attached to the Branch were exceedingly good detectives. (One of these girls, who left the force to get married to another member of the Detective Branch, was specially recalled for work during the war.)

In most big cases the work is done by a team, each member having a particular phase of the crime to cover. It is surprising how the smallest detail sometimes leads to the actual arrest and conviction of an offender. My task was to follow a chorus girl who was an unwitting accomplice. After many long hours of observation and fruitless enquiries, my lady assistant and I discovered the address we were looking for. This ended my part of the job. The two men were later sentenced to ten years' penal servitude.

In between these tasks, I was still frequently employed taking shorthand notes at meetings, all of which meant many late nights.

As a result of years of experience with shipping, I was again posted for duty at the docks, but this time my duties covered the docks at Silvertown and North Woolwich (commonly known as the Royal Docks) and the Pool of London, Surrey and East India Docks. It was a large area to cover and I was leader of a squad of ten men, answerable to an inspector at the Yard. In spite of the great extent of ground I had to cover, I loved this type of work. One day I would be jumping from barge to barge, or clambering over vessels loaded with timber, and the next day I would be boarding vessels in the orthodox way. I was frequently able to report useful information with reference to the construction of vessels from nations who were at that time contemplating going to war with us – information such as the special construction of capstan foundations and the extra thickness of the ship's plates. The movements of members of the crew also attracted very much attention from my colleagues and me.

One Saturday afternoon, I was checking passengers leaving Albert Docks for South America when I noticed one of the male passengers appeared to answer the description of a man who had been wanted for a large fraud in the City, committed about ten years previously. After the crime he had disappeared from the country. More on a hunch than anything else, I detained him until the arrival of an officer who could identify him. I say more on a hunch, because his description did not tally correctly with that of the wanted man. The one characteristic I was basing my suspicions on was that the man had a strange gait, the habit of a lifetime, and habits are difficult to change. He was identified by an officer connected with the original case and was brought before the City of London Magistrates. It was, however, impossible to find the original witnesses – some had since died – so he was released for lack of evidence. I was not disappointed at the result because the man had evidently lived down the past and had become a member of a well-liked section of Britishers in South America. He expressed surprise at my recognition of him, as he thought he had completely changed his appearance. I wished him luck when he left the country, about a month later than he had intended. I received another commendation for this capture.

Some weeks later, I was checking the odd passenger leaving on a small freighter for eastern Mediterranean ports. It was a quiet Saturday afternoon and this particular passenger was not very alert. After much discussion, without revealing that I was a police officer, and with the cooperation of the chief steward, who knew me, I discovered this man was engaged in the drug traffic for the Middle East. As a result of my enquiries and subsequent proof of his activities, he was later apprehended and finally sentenced.

The work in the Pool also entailed visiting vessels plying between Baltic ports, including Russia, and this country. There was always something of interest to be learned from these vessels.

In the evenings we took turns in covering the departure of the boat trains from Victoria to Paris. Some of the passengers on this special train known as the *Golden Arrow* always warranted some attention. While the Spanish Civil War was in progress, there were large numbers of left-wingers and sympathizers attempting to leave the country to join forces with the 'Reds' fighting in Spain. They left ostensibly as bona fide passengers, so there was no action that we could take to prevent their departure, but their identity proved useful for future occasions. Apart from these individuals, there were often interesting personalities from the film world travelling on the train. It was at this time I met Mary Pickford and Rosalind Russell for the first time in the flesh.

King George V had been in failing health for some time, and died. His son, the Prince of Wales, a very popular member of the Royal Family, became King Edward VIII, though he was never crowned as such. His association with Mrs Simpson caused quite a stir in political circles. Mr Baldwin, the Prime Minister, endeavoured to get the King to change his attitude towards this lady, but Edward was adamant, and his subsequent announcement over the radio regarding his decision to abdicate caused much discontent. The masses who loved him were opposed to the action taken by the government and would have willingly accepted the King's decision.

I was admitted to St Thomas's Hospital at this time with pneumonia, and had to be content to read all about it in the newspapers. I returned to duty just after Christmas and was appointed First Class Detective Sergeant. I was amused, when we appeared before the Selection Board, at the utterance of a colleague. Lord Trenchard, who was the Commissioner at that time, in addressing us said he had never made any mistakes. My colleague couldn't resist replying to the effect that he thought mistakes were the foundation of most successes. We were aghast at this statement, but Lord Trenchard was not a bit annoyed and merely laughed at the rejoinder.

I remained on duty at the docks for another year and then was recalled for further enquiry work.

The Civil War of Spain and the Italian brutalities in Abyssinia had completely changed the political situation. The Communists became more active and Oswald Mosley and his Fascists were holding political meetings all over London. The two factions were frequently at each other's throats and many street fights had to be quietened by the action of firemen with firehoses.

There was also at this time a smaller group who advocated social credit as a system of government; they became known as the 'Green Shirts' because of the shirts they wore. The Communists as always were attempting to cause disaffection in the workshops and were for ever lauding the Soviet system, while the Fascists were aping the followers of Mussolini and Hitler. They even raised their hands in greeting Mosley and shouted 'Hail Mosley'. Disorder at public meetings became commonplace and caused the uniformed branch much anxiety. It was at this time that William Joyce became well known to me. When he subsequently broadcast his propaganda from Germany during the war, his voice saying 'Germany Calling' was well known to every member of the Branch. The Fascists were a little easier to deal with and made no efforts to disguise their aims. As a shorthand writer, I was kept very busy and seldom got an evening or a Sunday to spend with the family. On top of this we were deluged with enquiries concerning the antecedents of the large numbers of refugees that were flocking to Great Britain from Germany. Altogether it was pretty hectic. Then came the historic visit of Neville Chamberlain to Munich and his arrival back in this country to make his fabulous speech 'No war in our time'. I still think he honestly believed what he said, and in any case we were in no position to force our views on any other nations, especially a great armed force like Germany. For several years rigid economy had been practised in Great Britain and much of it at the expense of our defences.

When 1939 was heralded in, it became obvious to everyone that war was inevitable and action was taken accordingly. Mussolini had for some time been bribing young Italians living in England by offering them a month's holiday free of expenses. They were then encouraged to declare their allegiance to Italy in time of war. A large colony of Italians resided in the London area and many of them had never taken out British papers. In addition there were considerable numbers of German citizens living and employed in this country. The political situation necessitated constant surveillance of the activities of these people. To make matters more complicated, the IRA became very active. They introduced themselves by causing explosions in postboxes in and around London and they even attempted to blow up bridges. It was difficult to tie in any particular individual with any crime, but our earlier enquiries – made years before – now began to prove useful.

It was not long before many participants in these new outrages were incarcerated in prison. The movement was well organized and each member had a particular task to perform. Most of these individual tasks were of an innocent character, but when connected with similar cases, there was no difficulty in proving guilty intentions. The strange thing about these activities proved to be that many of the saboteurs owed no allegiance whatever to Eire. They, of course, in the main, had Irish blood in their veins and were encouraged in their activities as members of the various Irish clubs around London.

The offences were for a time very trivial, but one day there was a serious outrage in Coventry and several people, innocent of any ill feeling against the Irish, were killed. Murder is a serious thing, and police activities were, as a consequence, hotted up and many arrests were made. The culprits were using very crude explosive methods, such as bombs which consisted of a rubber hot-water bottle with petrol and a small toy balloon, containing nitric acid, inserted in the neck. The object was that in a specified time the nitric acid would corrode the rubber and make contact with the petrol. The effect was enhanced by the addition of aluminium powder or sticks of gelignite. These ingredients were placed in attaché cases and deposited in various places. Sometimes another type of timing device was used; in these cases it was the innocent alarm clock. A copper contact was soldered on the alarm winder, which would in turn make contact with another piece of copper attached to a small pocket battery, usually a 4½-volt battery. When the suspects' houses were raided, in one we would find powdered aluminium, in another – black oxide, in another – alarm clocks, and so on. All perfectly harmless in themselves, but when used collectively, capable of becoming very destructive. The mere possession of any single one of these explosive agents did not constitute an offence. A conspiracy had to be proved before the law could take its course. A great deal of enquiry work was entailed, but often these enquiries failed to show a definite connection with any crime. After being engaged with these enquiries, I was switched to a different job, but still associated with the main issue.

The method I adopted cannot be related in full because I am still subjected to the rules of the Official Secrets Acts. I can, however, say that I became a temporary inmate of a remand prison and was able to associate with the men concerned with these outrages who were still on remand awaiting trial. I was also able to hear their conversations with outside friends. The men concerned were very astute and seldom gave away any information, but often parts of their conversation, when connected later with the utterances of others, supplied the key to certain acts. I was able to obtain much valuable information of this nature and other members of the gang were subsequently arrested and convicted. I was engaged on this job for many months and for some time after the outbreak of the war.

During August, just preceding the war, I was able to get a few weeks' holiday. I took the family down to South Wales and Bristol, where we spent many pleasant hours with relatives and friends. After leaving Bristol, we all expressed a wish to visit the Continent, so we bundled into the car one bright August day and set off for Folkestone. I parked the Morris in the dockyard at that town and bought tickets for a day trip to Boulogne. I knew many of the officials at that port and one of them, Mike Hunt, introduced me to a railway detective inspector who was travelling on one of his periodical visits to the Continent. We not only gained a good friend on the journey, but got first-class passage on the boat. We all travelled on the top deck. It was the first time that Clarice and the children had crossed the Channel, but not the first time they had been on a boat. We had often crossed the Bristol Channel on day trips from South Wales to the Devon coast.

There was a stiff breeze blowing up the Channel, and we all enjoyed the short crossing, in spite of the fact that some of the passengers were suffering from seasickness. We duly arrived at Boulogne and were conducted by our newly found friend to a very pleasant *estaminet,* where the children, Steve and Arthur, filled themselves with grenadine and citron. We partook of an excellent meal and then the proprietress introduced me to her son, a mine official from Lens, who was fortunately on holiday. He was a delightful young man, and suggested a trip around the town and surrounding countryside in his old car. It was exceedingly small, but we all squeezed in, including the inspector.

First we visited the picturesque church, then climbed the memorial to Napoleon, and then visited the nearby beauty spots and the British cemetery. Later we went on a shopping expedition, accompanied by our French friend. The assistant at the big store was apparently overcharging us, but Hubert quickly told the assistant off, and in fact we got a substantial reduction on the original prices. My knowledge of French at that time was quite elementary, but I gathered from the conversation that there were special increased charges for tourists.

We returned to the house and partook of another fine meal. Steve became a firm favourite of *Madame* during this visit, and we all promised to return the visit at a later date – unfortunately, we have never fulfilled this promise. After the usual goodbyes, we set off for the boat and were soon on our way back to England. I was the proud possessor of two very excellent bottles of cognac and was lucky to be met by a friend of mine in the Customs, who waived the duty. While we were still reliving this momentous holiday, the country became involved in the terrible war of 1939-45.

Just before the war commenced, Clarice left for Cornwall with Mrs Nall, whose husband had been called up for military service. Mrs Nall had a very young child and it was considered wise to get away from London for a time. Arthur had been evacuated with other schoolchildren to Cornwall, but Clarice did not know where he had gone at the time, while in fact he was only in the next village. Steve and I remained in London. I was still engaged on the special job, and Steve was still with her employers, a large building society office in the City of London.

5

The King and I

On the Sunday when the first siren sounded, Steve and I were in the garden talking to neighbours, but when the siren had ceased, we were left entirely alone. I had to attend to my job and left for duty at 2.00 p.m., while Steve stayed with friends nearby. Everyone expected a serious time to start, but in fact the first months of the war were very humdrum, but pleasant just the same.

After the first few weeks, I was returned to the Yard to help cope with the large number of enquiries which emanated from any scares. We were being inundated with phone calls from all over London from people who had seen something suspicious, or who believed acts of espionage were being committed. A large staff was employed for weeks dealing with these calls. Most of them were investigated — it is essential to enquire into anything that might sound or look at all suspicious. Some of these people saw significant features about innocent-looking orders for the delivery of flowers. They imagined the ordering of different flowers signified that a code was being used. The mysterious noises that frequently occur in water systems were turned into secret radio signals by the conscientious citizens. We would take turns at answering the phone calls and then would be detailed to make certain enquiries. Some of these special cases remain fresh in my mind today.

A phone call from north-west London one morning had to be investigated by me. The caller had said that she had seen a large number of SS uniforms being carried into a nearby house. I soon discovered that a film was being made in the vicinity, at the nearby Highbury Studios of a well-known film company, portraying the arrest of Pastor Niemöller and his subsequent incarceration in prison by the Nazis. The pastor was being played by Wilfred Lawson. The woman who had sent the message, being a stranger in London, knew nothing of the film studio, so when she saw the large number of uniforms, she was quite naturally suspicious. I was rather pleased with this case because I was invited to see some of the shots taken, and it was interesting to see how a film was produced.

Sometime later, I was sent to investigate a case of communicating with the enemy. Certain letters had been traced to an address in south-west London. It would have been useless to make a direct enquiry in such a matter, so I adopted the guise of an air raid warden. These gentlemen were empowered to enforce people to keep their windows completely dark at night. I kept observation on the house for several days and discovered that it was occupied by two women – one in her early forties and the other around 20 years of age. I recognized the younger woman as a member of, or an associate of, the British Fascist Party and I had frequently seen her in the company of William Joyce. (Joyce was subsequently identified as Lord Haw Haw and was executed as a traitor after the war.)

During my observation I had seen several members of the Fascist movement enter the house, so I decided to make a call myself. I was admitted to the house by the older woman, after I told her I was calling to draw her attention to the complaint about showing lights. I found her to be quite a gullible woman and pretended during my subsequent conversation that I was inclined to be sympathetic to the German cause. I had previously attended many Fascist meetings, so was well aware of their line of reasoning. We became very friendly and she confided quite a lot to me, and in fact she invited me to visit the house for a chat any time I was in the district.

During my visits, I got a good look at the whole of the interior of the house and by judicious conversation discovered the house to be a meeting place of prominent members of the Fascist Party. I also discovered that the older woman had a small son residing with German friends in Berlin and she was communicating with him via Switzerland, and also imparting information useful to Germany about other matters. I submitted this information to my superiors, but the case was left in abeyance, the reasons being only known to them. Later, when I was engaged on special duty with the King of Norway, the two women were arrested by MI5 and sentenced to long terms of imprisonment for espionage.

Clarice had by this time returned home and everything seemed to be very quiet and pleasant. The odd German plane came over to disturb us at night, but nothing serious happened. This state of affairs continued for some months, and the war became quite static – in fact it was referred to as the 'Phoney War'.

The spring of 1940 brought a more serious aspect with the sudden rush of German forces overrunning the Allied lines in France and the terrible toll of Dunkirk. Churchill made his famous speech calling upon everyone to defend the country against the German hordes. Defences were hurriedly erected at all vantage points and the Home Guard saw the beginning of a proud Army of old men willing to repel the enemy at the gates. Italy declared war on the Allies and for the next few weeks we were busy rounding up Italians for interrogation, and in some cases their internment. Whilst out with one of these round-up parties in June 1940, I was called to the Yard and instructed to take up the protection of the King of Norway. I was not at that time very keen to have this job, but on being told, I could not refuse, and went to King's Cross Station to meet the train bringing the King and his party to London.

There was a crowd of officials led by the King of England at the station to greet the King of Norway. I had no opportunity to announce myself at that time, but had to be satisfied with following the party to Buckingham Palace. I made my presence known to the proper official, in this case the naval liaison officer, Commander Eric Smith, and he instructed me to officially report to the King in the morning, and satisfied me that no movement would take place during the night.

I reported at the Palace at 10.00 a.m. on 9 June and was summoned to an audience with King Haakon of Norway. He was occupying the Grande Suite, situated at the northeast corner of the Palace and usually reserved for special guests. I was full of trepidation, but found later there was no need for any fear. As soon as I entered the royal apartment, the King, who was still attired in his Norwegian uniform, greeted me, and after shaking hands, introduced me to the Crown Prince, who also shook my hand. After giving me a resumé of what his movements would be, we chatted about the war in general, and on my expression of sympathy at the King's predicament, he replied, 'My misfortunes are great, but it is nothing compared with what is to happen.' He told me he would be confined to his apartment with matters concerning his government, and instructed me to meet him again in the morning.

Not having been engaged on this particular kind of duty before, I thought it advisable to wait in an ante-room. Here I met Jimmie MacDonald, King George VI's second valet. He gave me good advice, and then we chatted for some time about King George's visit to Canada, which had taken place earlier. I saw King Haakon go to dine with King George and the Queen, and then called it a day.

There was a suggestion that I should be accommodated in the Palace, but this proved unnecessary, because while the King was there he was sufficiently guarded by the police protecting the Palace. I returned home to Welling late in the evening and of course Clarice and Steve wanted to know what it was like to talk to a king. We were all very thrilled with this new experience and I must admit I felt quite proud.

The next day I returned to the Palace and was introduced

by Commander Smith to Colonel Nordlie, the King's ADC and Colonel Ostgaard, the ADC to the Crown Prince. Commander Smith had been attached to the King's party during the flight from the Germans in Norway, and the King was very fond of him. The King was engaged until lunchtime with his ministers, then he had lunch with King George and the Queen. After lunch, the King left the Palace in a car driven by Commander Smith, and I was invited to sit in the back seat. We drove to Richmond Park, where we left the car for a stroll amongst the trees. We frequently took these walks, but not always at the same spot.

On the second day, I was following the King at a short distance when he beckoned me to him and said, 'You might as well join Smith and me, then we can chat together.' From that time we were always together, unless the occasion arose when it was not convenient, for instance when he was with strangers to me, or in a place frequented by the public, and following was the best way to ensure his protection.

We spent Sundays attending the Norwegian Seamen's Church at Rotherhithe. On the first occasion we had to make use of one of the British royal cars, which was driven by a royal driver. My task, in addition to the usual protection duties, was to make sure the King arrived at the exact time. It was not difficult to do this on the first few Sundays. I knew the route well, but the subsequent bombing by the enemy made it very difficult and, in fact, as on one Sunday we were ten minutes late. This was not unexpected, as on the previous night London had suffered the heaviest bombing of the war. More of this later.

After breakfasting with the British royal couple, the King would return to his apartment in the Palace and there hold an audience with his various ministers and other callers. He would thus be engaged until lunchtime. Sometimes he would lunch with the King and Queen, but if not eating at the Palace, he would take lunch at either the United Services Club in Pall Mall or at the Norwegian Club in Trafalgar Square. No special arrangements would be made except for booking the normal lunch. King Haakon liked to be as inconspicuous as possible. He always wore uniform and, in the main, it was naval uniform. The King had been a serving officer in the Danish Navy, and was as a consequence very enthusiastic with anything connected with the sea. We usually travelled to these rendezvous by taxi. He would get the uniformed attendant at the Privy Purse door of the Palace to summon the taxi from the nearby rank. We would both ride together in the taxi. After lunch, I would hail another taxi and we would return to the Palace, where later in the afternoon, Commander Smith would arrive in his car. I would get into the back of the car and the King would ride in the front with Commander Smith.

On our first trips of this nature, we invariably travelled to Richmond Park, Roehampton or Commander Smith's private residence at Putney. We usually walked and talked for about an hour, then returned to the Palace. I always joined the party unless there were other VIPs present. I even joined the party if the King was alone with the Prince.

For the first few weeks in London, the King frequently renewed his acquaintanceship with old friends; some were Norwegian businessmen permanently residing in London. He went to Montpelier Square, the private address of Sir George Ponsonby, who managed the financial affairs of the Norwegian Royal Family in England, and, soon after his arrival in London, the King visited Queen Wilhelmina of the Netherlands, who was at that time residing at 82 Eaton Square; she later moved to the Stubbings, near Maidenhead.

On 25 June 1940, the Crown Prince left St Pancras for Dumfries in Scotland, where the Norwegians were endeavouring to form an army. The men, in the main, were seamen from whale catchers, who had decided to take up arms against the enemy. They were husky individuals and heavy drinkers, but seldom caused any trouble. The Chief Constable of Dumfries told me that when his men found a Norwegian very drunk, he merely placed him in a taxi and despatched him to the Norwegian camp, where the taxi driver was paid off and no trouble was caused to anyone. On

28 June, we went to St Pancras Station to meet the Crown Prince on his return from Scotland. The next day the King took lunch with Commander Smith and a friend at the Roehampton Club. We visited this club on many occasions and I was always provided with a very pleasant lunch. On the following Sunday, we attended the service at the seamen's church at Rotherhithe.

On 7 July 1940, the King was invited to lunch with Mr Anthony Eden at the Dorchester Hotel. Mr Eden met the King at the door. I spent the lunch period with Harold Battley, the detective sergeant attached to Eden; he was subsequently killed by enemy action whilst flying to the Yalta Conference.

Sometimes the King lunched with friends at the Carlton Hotel, just a quiet affair in the grill room. On one of these occasions he had no business to perform, so we discussed how we could spend the afternoon, and we all - the King, Commander Smith and myself - decided on a visit to the zoo. We went there in Commander Smith's car and after parking the car, we strolled around the grounds and the King wisecracked about the monkeys. He was very humorous at times. The next day we went to the Regal Cinema at Marble Arch to see a short documentary film. This visit was arranged by the Norwegian Government. I don't remember what the film was about, but I know the secondary film was a band affair, with lots of noise. This appeared to amuse the King, at least he told me it did when we were having our usual daily chat. On subsequent days we visited Claridge's Hotel, where the King took lunch with Prince Bernhard of the Netherlands. The next day we visited the Norwegian Red Cross at 27 Cadogan Square. The next day we were at a loss as to what to do, but after our usual chat, we decided to visit Madame Tussaud's Exhibition. The King visited all the sections and made some very humorous grimaces at the image of Hitler.

On the following day, we made one of our frequent visits to the private residence of Admiral Sir Edward Evans. The Admiral was then an official of the Air Raid Precautions in the London District. The King had dinner with Sir Edward and Lady Evans (she was the daughter of a Norwegian shipping magnate). Dinner was provided for me below stairs. Sir Edward always accommodated me on all our visits.

Later in the week, we went to Hampton Court and the King took tea with the Grand Duchess Xenia, a member of the Romanoffs of pre-Soviet days. Later we went to the London Palladium to see a show put on for charity. This was arranged by Sir Edward Evans and the King was introduced to Pat Kirkwood, the star of the show.

After returning from church on the following Sunday, we went to Warfield House, near Bracknell, the home of Sir Thomas Sopwith. Sir Thomas, known to all and sundry as Tommy, picked us up outside the Palace, and we were accompanied on this trip by Sir Edward Evans. We had a pleasant weekend with Sir Thomas and while there a strange thing happened to me. I was occupying a bedroom adjoining the King's. In the early hours of the morning I desired to use the toilet. To do so, I had to walk down a corridor. I made as little noise as possible, but much to my surprise I saw what I thought at that moment was the lady of the house standing at the top of the stairs. I turned to her and apologized for my movements, but of course received no reply. I discovered next morning that what I had thought was Lady Sopwith was merely a full-sized painting of the lady affixed to a panel on the stairs. In one of my lucid moments I told the King about my experience. He was highly amused and must have related the story to Sir Thomas, because on a subsequent visit to the house, he said to me, 'I will see you are not disturbed this time.'

Our visits to Admiral Evans's house became more frequent and we spent many more pleasant visits to Hampstead Heath.

On 30 July, we visited Greenwich Naval College. We travelled by road and were met by the Commander in charge of the college. I was tremendously impressed by the magnificence of the Grand Hall, where many famous people had dined, and was reminded of the works of Samuel Pepys. Queen Mary arrived later and joined the King and the senior officers at lunch. I had a very pleasant time with the junior officers in the wardroom. After a general inspection of the college, we boarded the Admiral's barge at the college slipway and travelled upriver to the Tower of London, where the King was met by the Constable of the Tower.

After a pleasant sojourn there – I was no stranger to the Tower, having spent many friendly hours with the beefeaters in their canteen called the 'Devil's Kitchen' when I was doing duty at the local docks before the war – the journey on the river was continued to Westminster Pier and then we boarded the waiting car and travelled to the Palace. It had been a very memorable day for me.

Early in August, we visited Wimbledon Common to see the effect of the recent bombing; this unfortunately was to be the forerunner of a bad period of bombing. Over the weekend of 3 August, we visited Bowdown House, a beautiful building situated in lovely woodland off Greenham Common, Berkshire. It was owned by Captain Dormer and his wife (she had previously been Lady Hambro, the widow of Sir Charles Hambro, the banker). This house was chosen as a possible residence for the King if he was required to leave London. Captain Dormer was the brother of the then Minister to Norway, Sir Cecil Dormer. We spent a very pleasant weekend in these delightful surroundings, and returned to Buckingham Palace on the Monday.

At 10.30 p.m. we left King's Cross for Edinburgh. Soon after our arrival, we left for Port Edgar and Rosyth, where the King inspected naval units with which Norwegians were associated. We returned to the Caledonian Hotel at 1.30 p.m. and later visited Craiglochart Hospital, where some Norwegians were being treated. We left Edinburgh on the 10.15 p.m. train and arrived at King's Cross at 8.00 a.m. next morning and then travelled back to Buckingham Palace.

The next few days we spent in the usual way – audiences

with the King and the usual lunches at various places, and the strolls across Hampstead Heath or down to the Roehampton Club.

On the following Sunday, the King made his usual visit to Rotherhithe Church and then to the Naval and Military Club for lunch. On 14 August, we again visited the Grand Duchess Xenia. On 16 August, after the usual lunch at the Norwegian Club, we, accompanied by Commander Smith, went to the zoo. On the way out, the air raid siren went, and because it was my duty to see the King came to no danger, I thought the best place to take him for shelter would be the nearest police station. So I took him to Albany Street. On our arrival, I introduced the King to the duty officer. He was a little overawed at first until I had reassured him that the King was a 'great guy' who liked nothing better than informality. While we were there, a policewoman came in and the King was anxious to make her acquaintance, so I called her over. The raid was fairly long, so we spent at least an hour at the station. The King told me next day that he had enjoyed his chat with everyone. Things were much about the same for the next few days.

On 21 August, we went to the Saville Theatre to see a special show arranged by Admiral Sir Edward Evans in connection with the ARP workers. On 25 August, the King, accompanied by the Crown Prince, went to St Olav's Church, Hart Street, EC. This was apparently in connection with some part of Norwegian history.

On 27 August, we went to the Plaza Cinema and at night left for Dumfries, where we arrived next morning. We went by car to Broomland, a large ancient house reputed to be connected with Robert Burns, the famous Scottish poet. The King inspected the Norwegian hospital at Troquer Mills, then went to Maxwelton House, where he inspected the Norwegian Artillery contingent, in the grounds. Maxwelton House is reputed to be where Annie Laurie, the heroine of the famous Scottish ballad, lived.

I was invited to the dinner given that night by the officers in honour of the King and his wonderful fight against the

German invaders. It was truly a great occasion for me. The food was austere, but the setting was brilliant. The tables were set in a horseshoe pattern; the King sat at the centre of the top table, surrounded by the Norwegian Commander – General Fleisher – and other senior officers. The other officers occupied the side tables and I was seated amongst them. Every now and again the chatter would be stopped as an individual officer rose, clicked his heels and addressed the King with the Norwegian salute *'Alt for Norge'*. It was a momentous event and the hours we spent later in the lounge drinking various toasts were most thrilling for me. During the course of the evening, the Crown Prince received a message stating that the Crown Princess Martha and the Prince and Princesses had managed to elude the Germans and were now on the high seas en route to the United States as guests of Mr Roosevelt.

The next day, the King inspected various units of the Norwegian forces and finally took the salute when the whole assembly marched past. Most of the men were raw recruits so far as fighting troops were concerned, being in the main crews from whalers who had volunteered to fight with the Allies. We then went to the local aerodrome, where the King inspected other units and a flight of British planes flew over in salute.

We returned to London on the 30th and later in the afternoon went for our usual drive around. The air raid siren sounded and we again had to take shelter and again we visited Albany Street Police Station. The following few days were spent in much the same way.

6

The War Gets Worse

On Saturday, 7 September, the King, accompanied by Commander Smith and myself, went to the News Cinema in Piccadilly. When we came out at 5.00 p.m., the air raid siren sounded, and though we did not know at the time, began the worst period of bombing we had experienced so far in the war. We returned to the Palace and Commander Smith went off duty. Machine-gun firing could be heard coming from high in the sky and German planes were seen in large numbers. They were mere dots in the sky. To get a better view of the situation, I accompanied members of the Palace staff to the roof. The scene was terrible, it looked as if the whole of the south-east section of the metropolis was on fire. Huge clouds of smoke could be seen rising in the sky over the docks. I was getting very anxious regarding Clarice, Steve and Arthur. The King informed me that he would not leave the Palace that evening, so I rushed off to Charing Cross Station.

On my arrival at the station, I discovered all the railway lines to Woolwich and Welling were damaged, and that no trains could run. I waited at the station for some time to endeavour to get a train somewhere nearer home. After what seemed an eternity, I boarded a train for Sidcup, knowing that I would have a walk of six miles before I eventually reached home. I didn't mind that, so long as I got home. I was terribly worried about Clarice and the family.

The raid was still on, but the train left Charing Cross and

we were soon within sight of the Surrey docks, from whence huge fires could be observed. Now and again huge explosions could be heard and debris could be seen blasted into the sky. By the time we arrived at Sidcup, the air raid siren sounded the 'all clear', so I set out to walk home as fast as my feet would take me. It was then about 11.00 p.m. and the sky was ablaze with stars. I was soon joined by another man who, like me, was bent on getting home as quickly as possible to his family. We arrived at Falconwood Station just as the air raid siren sounded the warning. Though we were both intent on proceeding on our journey, bombs or no bombs, we were forced by the air raid warden to enter the shelter by the station. We awaited our opportunity to get out and during some excitement caused by a nearby explosion, we made a run for it. My colleague went along the rail track, and I ran across the field – I had used this track for many months on my journey to and from the station. There were no lights, but I knew the footpath across the field so well that I could traverse it even on a foggy night.

I set off at a run and had hardly got halfway across the field when I fell down a huge crater which, by the fumes that pervaded it, must have been caused recently and was probably the result of the explosion we had just heard in the shelter. After what seemed an age, I picked myself up and clambered up the sides of the crater and continued my run across the field. The sky was full of German bombers making their way to the already big fires. Quite often a bomb would fall short and several fell in the immediate vicinity. However, after lots of ducking and weaving, I reached my house, which I was relieved to find still intact.

When I entered the house, there was no sign of Clarice or the kids, but this didn't worry me too much because Clarice had been in the habit of using neighbouring shelters when the raids were on – we had no shelter of our own. Steve had always remained in the house, because we always managed to persuade Arthur to accompany Clarice when she went to the shelter. Neither Steve nor I – or even Arthur – liked the shelters; we were not too brave, but preferred to remain above ground. I was therefore surprised not to find Steve in the house, but guessed the raiding had been so severe that she had at last been persuaded to take shelter. There was nothing I could do, so I got a chair fixed under the stairs and fitfully slept between the frequent tremors of bursting bombs.

The 'all clear' went at 5.00 a.m. and shortly after a knock came on the door. I answered it, and was greeted by a warden, who said, 'Are there any unexploded bombs in the garden?'

Feeling a little humorous at the time, I replied, 'Is there any garden left?' Soon after he had left, Clarice and the kids came in. I thanked God they were all OK!

On the Sunday morning, I took a hurried breakfast and attempted to get a train to London in order to resume my duties. The railroad gangs had endeavoured to keep open communications and, by taking devious routes, I was able to make it to the Palace. It meant travelling by train to Lewisham, then getting a lift on a truck and so on, until I got near enough to make it on foot.

In spite of the great fires and damage in the vicinity of the Seamen's Church at Rotherhithe, the King decided to attend divine service there. Though the buildings near the church had been almost completely destroyed and fires were still burning, the church was intact, except for all the windows being broken. After the service, we returned to the Palace and I remained on duty until 6.00 p.m., then I returned home. The homeward journey was still difficult; however, I reached home without any incident, but much later than usual. The night was interspersed with raids and the journey next day – Monday – to the Palace, took me over five hours.

The King had previously informed me of an appointment he had with his doctor at Baker Street, and because I had not arrived in time to accompany him, he left without me, but instructed the Palace footman to tell me to meet him at the address, which I would know. I made my way to the address and found the King had ended his appointment, and he was waiting for me to arrive. On the way back to the Palace, he told me bombs had been dropped on the Palace during the night and one – fortunately a dud – had dropped on the bathroom used by the King and the Crown Prince. I had noticed quite a bit of damage at the Palace when I first arrived in the morning – there were four large craters in the forecourt, and the wing on the right near Green Park had been completely destroyed. The rear of the Palace had been damaged and the swimming pool was partly destroyed.

It had been decided that if such a circumstance should arise, the King and his government would have to leave for another destination, and so as to make such a move quickly, we had equipped our cars with trailers to carry personal baggage and important documents. We had already practised this procedure. Owing to this latest raid, it was decided that that special day had arrived, so the King had been advised to leave as quickly as possible. He decided to go to Bowdown for the time being.

Now when I left home that morning, I had no idea that such a course would be taken and I was anxious to notify Clarice. I got permission from the King for the driver to take me home to collect a few belongings and inform Clarice of my departure. Unfortunately, when I arrived home, everyone was out, so, as time was short, all I could do was to leave a note saying I had to leave, but I could not tell Clarice where I was going, owing to security. I advised her to get away into the country and arranged that she should get in touch with the Yard when she wanted to communicate with me. I urged her, in the note, to get herself and the children away from London as quickly as possible. We arrived at Bowdown late in the afternoon and for the next few days I awaited news from Clarice.

Even though we resided away from London, the King still maintained touch with people in London and we visited the city every day.

One day I arrived back from London just after 6.00 p.m. and the maid at the house told me a female had asked to speak to me on the telephone, but she had arranged for the caller to speak again later. Somehow I guessed it was Steve, so I sat anxiously by the telephone until it rang. It was with great relief that I heard Steve's voice and I was thankful when I heard they had reached Reading and were staying there. Reading was only 17 miles away, so the driver, Cecil Rose, volunteered to take me there right away. Our meeting was one of the most joyous I have experienced.

The Norwegian Government had also moved out of London and were staying at Little Park, a large house on Greenham Common, about two miles from where the King was now residing. The bombing of London and the surrounding district carried on with all its intensity and the King, though anxious to get back to London, was advised to stay where he was for a while.

When not in London, the King would spend a great deal of time visiting with his government, and one afternoon he decided to attend the local cinema, the Forum. We frequently went to shows at this cinema, and as we tried to be as inconspicuous as possible, the King was seldom recognized.

One day, the Henderson Butlers (I forget what he was noted for) invited the King and the Crown Prince to take part in a shoot, so we spent a very pleasant afternoon at their home, Faccombe Manor. I was given a brace of pheasants and sent them to my mother, who was very fond of game. The lady of the house was a very pleasant woman, and I became very fond of her lovely black labrador dogs.

On Armistice Day we all went to London, and while the King was holding an audience at the embassy, Colonel Nordlie placed a wreath on the Cenotaph. In the afternoon the King and I went to 32 Green Street to look over a residence that was to be fitted out for him. This house was subsequently bombed beyond repair, so we never took up residence in London again. On 21 November, we again visited Sir Edward Evans and on the 23rd we had another day's shooting at Faccombe Manor. The King was driven to the various butts by Lady Henderson Butler and rode in the front of the car with her; I would sit in the rear with the lovely gun dogs.

On 12 December, we paid an official visit to Harwell Aerodrome. I was thrilled to see the great planes that were then bombing Germany and I had a lovely lunch in the officers' mess, while the King was being entertained by the station commander.

The evening of 23 December, we went to London to see the Crown Prince off to the USA. That was the first of his many flights across the Atlantic during the war. On Christmas Day, the King gave me a lovely set of gold cuff links and we visited Little Park, where he took lunch with the Norwegian Minister. On the last day of this eventful year, we visited Nortra Ships at Leadenhall Street, the headquarters of the Norwegian merchant vessels that were employed in the Allied cause.

On 11 January 1941, we travelled to Skegness, where the King was to inspect the personnel at the Royal Arthur Training Establishment, situated at Butlin's Holiday Camp, which had been taken over by the government for use by the forces. I had a very pleasant time, and was thrilled with the entertainment meted out to me by the officers. Unfortunately, the station was on the east coast and very near the shipping lane down the coast from Scotland, and as a consequence enemy raiders frequently disturbed the peace. The station orders were that everyone must take cover immediately the warning siren went. This order was strictly adhered to, and I became a little tired at having to take shelter, especially as the warning went about 20 times during the night.

On the Sunday, there was a march past, and the King, with senior officers, took the salute from a raised dais. After lunch, we drove out to Gundley Hall, the residence of Field Marshal Lord Massingbird. The King was met on the steps by the Field Marshal and after a short stroll round the grounds and a chat inside the house, we returned to the training establishment. The King dined with the commander of the station and I was invited to join the other officers to partake of an excellent dinner in the wardroom. I had previously arranged for Rose, our driver, to be accommodated with the petty officers, and he told me that they treated him very well. We left for London at 8.45 a.m. the next morning and arrived back at Newbury at 5.30 p.m.

On 22 January, the anniversary of my birth, we went by car to Portland, where the King was destined to officially accept four fast motor boats for the use of the Norwegian Navy. After the King had inspected the guard of honour and been introduced to the principal officers, we boarded one of the motor vessels and went for a trip down the English Channel. The speed of these vessels was terrific and I enjoyed their wonderful manoeuvrability. Dummy depth charges were fired to demonstrate the quickness. After the trip, we landed at Weymouth and the King took lunch with the station commander and I was invited to join the other officers at a very fine lunch. We returned to Newbury later in the day – everybody having enjoyed it immensely.

On 30 January, the King was invited to visit the Officers' Club at the Grosvenor Hotel, Park Lane. We arrived in London at the usual time and after conducting his business, which this time was a meeting of the Norwegian Government, or Storting, the King took lunch with the minister at Norway House.

When I had made sure he was safely ensconced, I made one of my regular visits to the Yard and then returned to meet the King after his lunch. We took a taxi to a hairdresser in St James's Street. I was waiting outside while the King was getting his hair trimmed, when the air raid warning went. Shortly after the warning had stopped, I spotted seven German planes flying over the Houses of Parliament, and thinking they were too close to be pleasant, I dived down the steps of the hairdressing establishment. I found myself quite close to the King, who was being attended by the tonsorial artist. He laughed when I excused my presence, but replied, 'This is the best place, so long as they don't drop a direct hit.' The raiders flew overhead and made for the Edgware Road district, where shortly afterwards exploding bombs could be heard.

The odd small raid was now quite a common occurrence,

and unless there was any danger of a bomb dropping in the immediate vicinity, people merely glanced into the sky and then went on their way – they seldom bothered to enter the shelters. Personally, I preferred to be in the open; I dreaded being buried alive – I had not forgotten my experience of the First World War.

Early the next day, we were back in London again and were soon making the usual calls, and we continued this programme for the next few weeks. We made our usual Sunday visit to Rotherhithe Seamen's Church and occasionally visited the cinema at Newbury in the afternoons which were dull. The Crown Prince used to accompany us to the cinema, but he invariably walked back to the house alone – it was quite a step too, about four miles.

In March 1941, British forces, together with some Norwegians, raided the Lofoten Islands of Norway, and after wrecking some German installations, they returned with large numbers of Norwegian civilians and some prisoners. The civilians were housed at various places in Central London and, as was usual in such cases, the King desired to talk with them and reassure them that he and his government were still very interested in their welfare.

On 8 March, we went to the Royal Hotel, Woburn Place, where the King spoke to a large audience of people. He was greeted most enthusiastically by everyone. He mixed amongst the people and talked to one and all.

On the 13th, we visited Admiral Sir Edward Evans's residence in Cadogan Square, where we had lunch. I was always provided with lunch at the house. The King made a point of arranging my lunch before he sat down to his own.

On the 15th, we went to Abingdon aerodrome to inspect more bombers. Some of the members of the crews were Norwegians.

We were back in London again on the 16th, to make a special visit to the church at Rotherhithe, then to Sir Edward's for lunch. Later we went to the Central Station of the London Fire Brigade to see a demonstration, then later to Grosvenor House Hotel, where the King spoke to the assembly.

On 27 March, under the auspices of Sir Edward, we visited the Paper Cup Company factory on the Great West Road at Bedford, to witness a demonstration of first aid by the girls at the factory after a mock raid; then, accompanied by the Admiral, we went to Wandsworth Town Hall, where the King was met by the Mayor of Wandsworth and later inspected the ARP personnel. He later lunched with the Mayor and the councillors. It was well organized, and I had some interesting chats with members of the staff.

From here we went to Clissold Park, Stoke Newington, in company with the leading members of the ARP, together with sections of the Fire Brigade or National Fire Service, as they then were known. We also visited Hornsey Town Hall and Finsbury Park. Herby Morrison accompanied the King on this tour of inspection and he seemed very impressed with Herby's sincerity. The King told me later, during one of our many walks, that he thought Mr Morrison was a very upright man, and he laughed when I said, 'Naturally, he is the son of a policeman.' Before the King left the district, he christened a new fire engine 'King Haakon'. The ceremony was greeted with huge cheers from the crowd that had assembled.

On the last day of the month, the King was an honoured guest at a lunch given by the Pen Club at Frascattis, a well-known restaurant.

On 5 April, we visited Westcroft Park, Chobham, the residence of the boss of Serpell's Biscuit manufacturers. I cannot remember what connection this visit had.

The 6th found us at Eddington Park, Hungerford. It was a weird old house, and I shall always remember the place well, because of the actions of the butler. He was a mean-looking individual. He offered me a drink, as was the custom when visiting these places, but it looked a frightful colour, so I declined. It was as well that I took this action, because I discovered after a conversation with the housekeeper that he emptied the contents of various used bottles into a decanter and offered this concoction to his guests – sometimes with very bad results. Pretty potent stuff, I should imagine, considering it consisted of whisky, gin, brandy and anything else that might be handy.

The next day, the King was invited to make an inspection of the Admiralty 'Ops' room. Owing to the extreme secrecy necessary in connection with such a place, I had to be content with staying in the outer room. The King later discussed his visit with me, but with his usual tact, left out the very secret details. He obviously had no intention of breaking faith in spite of the fact that he trusted me implicitly. He always entrusted me with the destruction of secret documents. I used to lock myself in the furnace room and destroy everything by fire. The King once said to me, 'You know, Coates, a secret is no longer a secret when more than two people know of it.'

On 12th we visited Stoneydene, Headley Down, Hampshire, the residence of a prominent Norwegian. The King had dinner here and I was invited to take a meal with the housekeeper.

On the night of 14 April at about 2.00 a.m., whilst we were at Bowdown, I was awakened by the police patrol, who thought he had seen a parachutist alighting in the grounds of the house. I hurriedly collected members of the household and we searched the grounds very thoroughly, but even though I became enmeshed in a blackberry thicket, we failed to find any trace of a parachute.

We continued the search until daylight, but it was not until 8.00 a.m. that we discovered the object of the search was a meteorological balloon. This episode caused a great deal of laughter, but the search was very necessary because at that time several spies had been discovered to have landed by parachute in the country.

On the 16th, after the usual business in London, we were driving back to Newbury, and just as we entered the Colnbrook Bypass, I had occasion to look at the speedometer of the car and discovered it registered 75 m.p.h.

Thinking it was much too fast, I informed the driver. Unfortunately, before my remarks could register, we were approaching a humpback bridge and as we crested the hill, I saw a coal truck just turning to enter a gate on the right-hand side of the road. It was too late to avoid a crash of some kind. Our driver thought he could not brake in time, so he endeavoured to drive the car between the rear of the truck and the kerb. The speed was, however, too great for that manoeuvre to be successful, so as the car swerved, the rear tyre hit the kerb and burst. The driver, with great skill, managed to steer the car along the grass verge, but we hit a concrete pylon in the middle of the grass verge. These pylons were placed at intervals along the sides of wide roads to prevent aeroplanes from landing. On the left of the grass verge there was a drop of about 30 feet into boggy ground. The impact on hitting the pylon caused the front of the car to concertina, and as a consequence the doors became jammed.

Between the driver and myself and the other occupants of the car there was a glass screen. The King and his ADC sat on the rear seat, but Commander Smith was sitting on a tip-up seat immediately behind the glass screen. I, and the driver, had sensed the danger and tensed ourselves for the impact, but Commander Smith was dozing at the time, and on the impact he smashed his face against the screen; at the same time, his right hand, holding his cane, struck backwards, hitting the King on the nose. The driver of the truck managed to free us, but of course he had no idea of the identity of the occupants of the car. Commander Smith was suffering from shock and a fractured nose. I always carried a first aid dressing with me, so I was able to temporarily dress his nose, which at the time looked ghastly. With the aid of the local police, who were summoned on my instruction by the driver, I arranged an ambulance and Commander Smith was taken to Slough Hospital, while another car was obtained for the King's transport to Newbury.

We proceeded on the journey as soon after the accident as possible, but we stopped at Slough to enable the King to make a personal enquiry at the hospital regarding Commander Smith's condition. Whilst the King was stopping at the hospital, he heard the ADC say to me that he thought Rose was driving too fast, but the King interrupted the conversation and said, 'I don't think so.' He was always so kind and considerate and avoided any complaints about anyone.

On 24 April, the Crown Prince returned from his visit to the USA. Apart from the regular routine of visiting London, we made no special visits until 17 May, when the King again visited Grosvenor House Hotel, in connection with a gathering for the benefit of the Allied Officers Club. While the proceedings were being conducted in a kind of annex with no roof above the floor, a raid commenced and it was not long before bombs were dropping in the vicinity – some less than 200 yards away. The guns in Hyde Park were barking and the noise was terrific. The hostess of the club suggested I advise the King to go to the shelter, but of course the King would not do so, and he carried on as if nothing was happening. He later told me, when I mentioned that the principals of the club were anxious that he should take shelter, 'I could not do that, it would have set a bad example, especially as the shelter would not have been large enough to hold everyone present.' He was indeed a brave and considerate man.

The Crown Prince went to Portland on 10 June – it had been suggested that the King should also go, but the itinerary was changed at the last moment. The King went to Ramsbury Manor on 14 June, and on the 15th to Jacob Wells, Guildford, the residence of Sir Cecil Dormer. It was difficult getting across country during these days because all the road signs had been removed. It was essential that the King arrived at his destination on time, so I overcame the difficulty by advising the Yard of my movements and they in turn enlisted the aid of the local police. The King liked everything to be done in an unostentatious way, so I would obtain a route from the AA and then arrange for guidance at difficult spots. The local police would arrange for a motorcyclist to be at the awkward junctions. The cyclist, being acquainted with the number of our car, would lead us without showing any signs of recognition, and on a nod from me, he would disappear and we would carry on alone. The King would invariably instruct his counsellors to thank the police after the journey. With this system prevailing, we had very little trouble in arriving at our destination on time, and without any difficulties arising.

7

Visiting the Famous

During the war, the Dowager Queen Mary resided at Badminton House, the residence of the Duke and Duchess of Beaufort. She was closely associated with the King, and it occurred to me that he would be visiting that house very frequently. I knew the route quite well, with the exception of a few miles off the main road; I had covered this route hundreds of times before, as it was the main road to Bristol.

We made our first visit to Badminton on 22 June. On arriving at Chippenham, I discovered with dismay that we would have to go faster if we hoped to be on time – anyway, we made Badminton at the allotted time: 1.15 p.m.

We visited a pig farm on 28 June, which was owned by a Dane; it was called Hansen's Farm at Cholsey, near Wallingford. It proved to be an interesting visit as the methods of breeding were right up to date.

Later in the week, we made another visit to Ramsbury Manor. I never can remember who lived at this palatial old building. Most of the people we visited were, or had been, connected with Norwegian affairs. Some of the people were ex-diplomats.

On 3 July we made the first of many visits to a concert. I detested these concerts; I never could appreciate the music – they bored me to tears. This particular concert was a charity affair held at the Dorchester. The women in attendance appeared to be enraptured with the 'noise', but the menfolk seemed to be sleeping.

On 5 July, I registered at Newbury Labour Exchange under the Registration for Employment Order 1941. This Act ensured that every member of the community was engaged in useful work for the war effort. It of course hardly affected me, as I was a police officer with special duties.

We visited Barnwell Manor, Northampton, the country house of the Duke and Duchess of Gloucester, on the 12th we stayed the night there. It was a pleasant day when we arrived and the Duke was out with the harvesters. I toured the ruins of Barnwell Castle, which was within the estate, and on the Sunday, the King accompanied the Duke and Duchess to the local church for divine service. It was a delightful country church. I later saw the young Prince in his perambulator and chatted with his nurse. Later in the afternoon I accompanied the Duke's police officer, a member of the Metropolitan Police uniform branch, to the local police at Oundle. We returned to London later in the day and then to Newbury in the evening.

On 21 July, we went to London as usual and at 7.20 p.m. caught a train from Euston for Inverness, where we arrived next morning at 9.50 a.m., then by car to Invergordon, where the King visited some Norwegian Air Force officers and men. Later we went to Carbisdale Castle, Culrain, Ross-shire, the residence of a Mr Salveson, a shipping magnate. The castle was built for the Dowager Duchess of Sutherland but had been bought by Mr Salveson. While staying at the castle, I was sleeping in a large room immediately beneath the clock tower – the thump of the clock when striking sounded very eerie. We visited the Norwegian Brigade HQ, accompanied by Colonel Sir John Aird, who was at one time the ADC to the Prince of Wales but during the visit was the liaison officer between the British and Norwegian forces in Scotland. The General i/c of the Scottish Command was General Thorne. He had a very squeaky voice and always carried a type of shepherd's crook. I discovered he was a very charming gentleman. We paid visits to the various units of the Norwegian forces at Tain, Edderton and Dingwall.

On 24 July, we attended manoeuvres up in the mountains. It was thrilling because the troops were attacking their position with live ammunition, so every care had to be taken. Even so, there were casualties. I enjoyed the lunch, which was in the open air and consisted of sandwiches with hot coffee, partaken in the company of the King and the Commanders.

At night there was a special dinner laid on, and I thoroughly enjoyed the view of the guests assembling in the grand hall of the castle and then walking in pairs down the hall, behind a brilliantly dressed Scottish piper. After the guests were assembled in the dining hall, the piper marched around playing various airs on his pipes, and before being dismissed, downed a large glass of neat whisky. I later chatted with the piper, who was actually a local doctor who apparently had spent many pleasant years in London, and had the pleasure of dining with him in an adjoining hall. The whole scene was magnificent and reminded me of what medieval days must have been like. The Duke and Duchess of Sutherland were present at the dinner. After the dinner, we left the castle by car for Inverness, where we boarded a train for Dumfries, arriving at 9.10 a.m. on 25 July.

Whilst at Dumfries, we visited Drumlanrig Castle, the house of the Duke and Duchess of Buccleuch and the birthplace of the Duchess of Gloucester. Later we visited Maxwelton House, Goldilea and Newlands Hospital.

We left for London at 11.30 p.m. from Dumfries and arrived at 8.50 a.m. next day, then on to Newbury, where we arrived at 5.30 p.m.

On 6 August, we went to Fawley Court, a large country house just beyond Henley-on-Thames. This was a very secret visit and my instructions were to get the King to Henley centre, where we would be met by a motorcyclist. We rendezvoused with the cyclist and followed him to the house. The King was very bad-tempered this particular day, a most unusual occurrence for him.

On arrival at the house I discovered it was a special training school for parachute and commando troops. All kinds of exhibitions were arranged, including the placing of limpet mines on ships' sides and the destruction of dock installations. In all, it turned out to be a very interesting day. We returned to Newbury later.

On 9 August, we visited Scrubbs Hill, Sunningdale, where the sports meeting of Nortra Ships was in progress. The King mingled with the contestants and then we had a meal in a large marquee in the grounds.

We paid another visit to Warfield House, the home of Tommy Sopwith, on 16 August, and stayed there for the weekend. On the Monday morning we left with Tommy Sopwith for London, but made a stop at the Fairey Aircraft works on the West Road, where the King was conducted over the factory by Tommy. The King was later shown, and I had a glimpse of, the famous fighter plane of the war, the Hurricane. At that time its construction was a great success.

On the 19th we visited Hollow Dene, Frensham, Surrey, the residence of a prominent Norwegian.

On the 23rd, we went to London and visited the Gaumont Film Studios at Ealing, where we saw shots being taken of the picture of the torpedoing of the *Demetrius* – the oil tanker that was cut in half and was yet brought to port by a skeleton crew. At 2.15 p.m., we went by car to Skegness on another visit to the Royal Arthur Training Establishment. I was tickled to death on our arrival outside the guard-room. I met the duty officer and instead of conducting us to the rendezvous, he got into the car and occupied my usual seat. I was left temporarily stranded, but the King, always equal to such occasions, directed me to sit inside the car with him. Later this officer apologized to me, but his subsequent entertainment was a just reward.

After dinner in the wardroom, we all went to a grand concert given by ENSA.

On the 24th we attended church parade and later the King took the salute. After lunch we visited Gundley Hall, and again met Field Marshal Massingbird. After dinner at Royal Arthur, I visited Mr Butlin at his office in Skegness.

We left Skegness at 8.45 a.m. next day for London and Newbury, where we arrived at 6.00 p.m.

The first day of September we went to Roehampton Club and later to the Ritz. The King stayed at the embassy for the night, so I made one of my very infrequent visits home to Welling.

On the 2nd, the King visited Tavistock House, Woburn Place, where large numbers of Norwegians were staying. We returned to Newbury later in the day.

On the 12th, lunch with Admiral Evans, and after lunch we attended a special show put on by the ARP at the Palladium. We went backstage and met some of the artists, including Miss Pat Kirkwood.

On 16 September, the King attended the coming-of-age service for King Peter of Yugoslavia held at St Paul's Cathedral. All the heads of the Allies were present and the ceremony was very impressive. They all formed up in the vestibule and marched in pairs up the aisle. The trumpets were sounded from the gallery.

Then on 22 September, we went to His Majesty's Theatre in the Haymarket to see a show put on in aid of the WVS.

On the 25th, we went to Claridge's, where the King dined with King George of Greece. It was nice to meet Bill Smith again (he had been attached to the King of Greece for some time).

Another shoot was attended by the King at Faccombe Manor on the 27th.

On 2 October, we went to the Czechoslovakian Legation, where the King had a long chat with President Benes. On the 8th we visited Lady Constance Butler at her house, The Cottage, at Taplow. On 10 October, we left Reading on the 2.15 p.m. train for Plymouth and stayed at Admiralty House. There was a raid during the night, but nothing untoward happened. I enjoyed my dinner with the Admiral's coxswain. On the 11th we visited Norwegians in barracks and then went to Mill Bay Docks. We left at 5.00 p.m. by road for Dartmouth. I was allotted a berth with one of the officers, whose main duty was the marshalling of ships leaving for convoys up the Channel. I had a long chat with the commander in charge of the college, where we were to stay for the rest of the weekend.

For a week or more I had had a huge carbuncle on the back of my neck, and this had just begun to give me trouble. The commander instructed me to visit the sickbay, where I was attended by an orderly. After treatment I returned to the wardroom for dinner and later was treated by the Surgeon Commander. I then returned to the wardroom, and in spite of the pain of my neck, enjoyed the fun.

The officers were enjoying themselves, as all naval personnel know how to do so well. Every new guest was required to lie on his back on a rickety heap of chairs piled on top of a table and reaching almost to the ceiling. From the top of this precarious perch, the victim was supposed to draw something interesting on the ceiling. The Crown Prince was the special guest this evening, so he was required to perform the ceremony. He was a good sport and raised no objection, and immediately took up his position on the top of the chairs, finally drawing a beautiful design of criss-crossed flags of England and Norway on the ceiling. The reward was drinks all round. In the excitement of the evening, I had forgotten all about my carbuncle. On the Sunday morning, I again attended the surgery and was again treated by the Surgeon Commander.

I then witnessed the King inspecting Divisions performed by the cadets of the college on the wonderfully situated parade ground. We later toured the college grounds and the harbour works.

Early on Monday morning saw me again at the surgery, and the surgeon managed to cut out the core of the carbuncle and patched it up for the journey back to Newbury. It hurt damn bad, but I was glad to get it out. We left just after breakfast by car for Newton Abbot and then by train to Reading. We again visited Sunningdale on the 21st.

On 2 November, we visited Badminton and were

entertained to the usual lunch – I mean the driver and myself. We always had the same meal – venison, when in season, and chicken when venison was out of season. It was a very interesting dining hall surrounded by glass cases containing stuffed wolves that at one time had roamed the countryside.

On 3 November while in London, we visited a show put on for the police at the Coliseum Theatre. On the 8th, in the midst of the usual visits to London, we visited Bridley Manor, Worplesdon, Surrey. On 23 November, we visited the residence of a one-time ambassador at Weir House, Alresford, Hampshire.

On the 25th we visited the British Medical Association at Tavistock Square and on the 26th we went to Romany at Wentworth, Virginia Water, to take lunch with the Polish President. It was a grand affair and I enjoyed the spicy foods and the drinks that accompanied them. Everything was served with the graciousness so akin to the Poles. On the 27th the King lunched at Lloyd's, Leadenhall Street. I was thrilled to see the huge vaults.

On 28 November, we left Newbury at the usual time and were travelling through Reading towards London when at the top of Shepherds Hill, just outside the town, a pedal cyclist turned from a side road right into the path of our car. Though we were travelling at a moderate speed, being still in a built-up area, his body was tossed into the air and his head hit the top of the hood. I knew in an instant that he had been killed. Rose stopped the car at once and I rushed to the back of the car just in time to see the cyclist, an old man, expire. It was an awful sensation and for a moment I wondered what I should do, but fortunately I collected my senses and entered the nearby police station. They took charge of the affair and I promised to keep Rose in my custody until we returned later in the day, when I would bring him to the station for his report. We were allowed to proceed on our journey, which for the rest of the time was rather saddening.

On our return to the house in the evening, I went with Rose to the station, where we made our reports. I had already made an official report at the Yard. The inquest was detailed for 1 December. I was relieved for the day by Percy Fife. Rose was exonerated at the inquest, but his future as a driver was now at stake. He continued to drive and on 2 December we went to London and visited a special show held for the benefit of the ARP charwomen at the Princes Theatre, Shaftesbury Avenue. On the 8th we made another visit to Grosvenor House Hotel.

On the 11th the Prince left for the USA. A Norwegian exhibition at the Mayfair Hotel was visited on the 12th.

On the 18th, the King made a special recording at the BBC for Christmas greetings to Norway on the 25th. After the broadcast, the King went to Euston Station, where we boarded a train for Glasgow and arrived there at 8.50 a.m. the next day. We stayed at the Central Hotel and visited the City Chambers for lunch. It was quite a grand occasion and we were all presented with an artistic book about Glasgow.

We later visited the Clydeholm Ship Building Yard, where the King launched a new ship named *HM Haakon VII*. After we visited the Seamen's Club in Argyle Street, we left Glasgow for London at 10.30 p.m. and arrived at 10.00 a.m. next day.

On the 25th, we went to church at Rotherhithe and then had lunch at the Savoy before leaving for Newbury.

On 1 January 1942, we attended a concert at the Albert Hall. The concert was a charity affair and was attended by many VIPs. The King and Queen of England and young King Peter were present. It was interesting to see the group together. I always wished I had a camera on these occasions. The concert, as usual, bored me.

By now the insurance company had refused to accept Rose as a risk, so that meant his retirement from driving. It was arranged that a young Norwegian should take his place, and Per Winther Leversen was chosen. We picked him up at the embassy. He was a fairly good English-speaking Norwegian, and I discovered that he had been for a short time engaged with police work in Norway, but had managed to escape, with others, in a small fishing boat to England. He was a very nice and clean youngster and was well liked by everyone.

We went to the Grosvenor Hotel again on the 12th and on the 17th we attended a wedding at St Saviour's Church, Walton Place. I forget whose wedding it was, but I think it might have been King Peter of Yugoslavia.

The Duke of Connaught died and on 23 January 1942 the King of Norway attended the funeral at Windsor Castle. It was a very impressive ceremony, which was attended by most members of the Royal Family. It was rather thrilling for me to come in such close contact with royalty.

The remainder of the month was taken up with the usual journeys to London, practically daily occurrences, when apart from the business that the King conducted at the embassy, meant the occasional visit to residences of friends and acquaintances of the King. These visits were mostly of an impromptu nature and many of the people we visited were unknown to me. I would meet the King after lunch and he would then give me an address where he wanted to go. I would call a taxi and we would make our way together. It sometimes happened that I would be accommodated with a cup of tea with a lady's maid, while the King would be entertained by his host or hostess. On some of these visits we had to make use of the service lift; I usually found the way to operate it. We always made our final rendezvous at the Royal Yacht Club for the return journey to Newbury.

Rose, on leaving the service of the King, had managed to get the managership of the Regal Cinema in Newbury, and the King was highly amused on our next visit to this cinema when Rose showed us to our seats. We always sat together; even the driver was accommodated – in fact we would wait until he had parked the car before proceeding to our seats.

On 8 February 1942, we visited Badminton. When we arrived at the house, after depositing the King at the front door, where he was invariably greeted by Queen Mary, the King would suggest a time for leaving and then we would take our lunch with the butler, and after lunch, Per and I would either stroll through the spacious parklands or chat with the members of the army detachment.

On this particular occasion, Clarice was staying with her sister at Bristol and Per suggested that we pay a flying visit to that city. Bristol was about 20 miles from Badminton, and with the powerful car at our disposal, the journey could be accomplished very quickly. It was with great pleasure that we met Clarice and Madge, and after a quick cup of tea we persuaded the ladies to come back with us to Cirencester, where they could get a bus back to Bristol. We arrived back at Badminton in good time and everyone had had a pleasant afternoon.

During the winter months, a large aerodrome had been in course of construction on Greenham Common. This was to be used as a bomber base by the American Air Force, so it was obvious the King could not stay much longer in residence at Bowdown. It had been suggested sometime earlier that the King could with advantage be accommodated a little nearer London, and Foliejon Park, near Windsor, had been noted as the possible choice.

We made our usual visit to London on 19 February, and on the return journey we visited Foliejon Park. It was a spacious house situated in a large park – an ideal residence actually because of its quiet situation. The King thoroughly examined the house and appeared to be pleased with what he had seen. We later resumed our journey to Newbury.

On the following Saturday, the King visited Chilham Cottage, Itchen Stoke, Hampshire. Since I had been living at Newbury, I had had my car brought from home and found it very useful for picking up Clarice when she visited me; Per also made use of it at times. The King knew I had my car at the house, so while on our usual walk through the grounds, he suggested that as I knew the route to Foliejon, he thought it would be a good idea if I preceded the King's car and led the procession to the new house.

On 17 March 1942, we set off, with me in the lead, for Foliejon, where we arrived without incident some 60 minutes later. It was amusing to me and very unorthodox. The journey to London after our move to Foliejon was shortened by about 45 minutes, but we still left the house at the same time each morning.

The King was invited to inspect the Empress Memorial Hall at Salmon Lane on 19 March. I had been to this place many times before when doing duty at the nearby docks. The King enjoyed his visit – he always made everyone feel so at ease and of course seamen always held a special place in his heart.

On the 21st we visited the National Portrait Gallery to see some exhibition of service drawings. On the 22nd we visited the church at Rotherhithe and again visited there on 5 April.

On 7 April, we went to Reading Station, where we boarded the 8.45 a.m. train for Temple Meads, Bristol. We were met at the station by the Lord Mayor and then driven to the Guildhall, where after signing the visitors' book, we partook of sherry (Bristol Milk) with the Lord Mayor and local VIPs. Later we drove out to the Bristol Aircraft Factory, where we saw the various processes in the manufacture of aircraft of the famous Beaufighters. After lunch in the factory mess, we saw a special flight of fliers. While I was there with the King, Bob (my nephew) saw me; I didn't know at that time that he was employed there – it was before his call-up.

We then drove out to the large underground factory near Corsham, which was then under construction. It was a huge place, from which large quantities of local stone had been removed. After a very hectic day we drove finally to Badminton, where we stayed the night.

On the following morning, we caught the 9.45 a.m. train from Temple Meads for Birmingham. We made the usual call to the Council House with the now familiar speeches by the Lord Mayor and other local dignitaries.

After leaving the Council House, we drove to Armstrong Vickers factory and saw some of the construction taking place. These visits were always of great interest to me. So often do we use things, but have no idea how they are made;

once you have seen the various processes they at once assume greater interest. We then visited Dunlops huge tyre factory. The manufacture of tyres is another interesting process, and I marvelled at the adeptness of the men changing tyres so rapidly with what seemed very little effort.

After another busy day, we drove to Himley Hall, the home of the Earl of Dudley. (I believe this huge mansion is now one of the regional headquarters of the National Coal Board.) I was allotted spacious accommodation for the night, but found it very cheerless and was glad to be able to spend most of the evening with the butler, who had quite a lot of stories to relate.

On the 9th, we left Himley Hall about 8.35 a.m. after a very fine breakfast, and caught the 8.58 train from West Bromwich to Liverpool, where we arrived at 10.00 a.m. We toured the Mersey docks and the King spoke to several seamen and then we went to the Adelphi Hotel for lunch. After lunch we visited the Western Approaches Naval Headquarters. The King was shown around by the Commander-in-Chief and was later introduced to Lord Derby – what a huge man he was. I can see him getting into his car now – it looked as if it would collapse with his weight. Apart from his huge bulk, he appeared to be a very fine humorist and everything he said was met with loud peals of laughter. After the usual introductions, we drove to the house of Lord Derby – Knowsley Hall – a huge mansion standing in a beautiful park. The grounds had already received attention from the bombers, but there appeared to be no serious damage to the house itself. I was surprised to see that there was accommodation for quite a large staff of workers on the estate. I was entertained by the butler and found Lord Derby himself a very generous man.

We left early next day by train from Liverpool to Sheffield. We were met at the station by the Lord Mayor and driven in the civic cars to the Civic Centre. The King was welcomed by huge crowds of cheering people. The Civic Centre was very interesting and the staff attended to my comforts in an admirable way. We toured the English Steel Corporation Troubite Works and witnessed many processes, including the opening of a steel retort – the flow of the white hot metal had to be seen through special glasses. During this visit, the King was accompanied by the Earl of Harewood. At the final goodbye, he was presented with a special gold penknife.

I was astounded to see some very frail-looking girls doing various turning jobs on a huge gun. One of these girls told the King she was a mannequin in private life. I noticed that women can become experts at almost everything, if they have a will to do so.

After driving through a part of the city that had been heavily attacked by enemy aircraft, I was astonished to see how quickly the local authorities got everything moving again. We left Sheffield at 5.10 p.m. for Marylebone, where we arrived at 9.40 p.m., and then home to Foliejon.

On 13 April, the King was invited to tour the Ministry of Home Security. The Ministry was housed in a large underground set of offices – a huge labyrinth of rooms, well lit in spite of being so many feet below the surface of the street.

Biggin Hill Fighter Station was visited on the 14th. There were one or two Norwegian pilots stationed at this very important aerodrome defending London. We arrived early and took breakfast with some of the pilots who were later to perform flying duty over the English Channel. The King chatted to several of them and then we adjourned to the 'Ops' room. By the aid of radio we were in constant touch with the flyers throughout the operation. It was all very thrilling to hear the pilots shout 'Tally ho' and then to hear them describe their encounters with the enemy.

We heard one pilot set off after three enemy fighters, but he apparently was hit just as he was about to break off the engagement. We heard him shout 'Mayday', and after what seemed an eternity, we heard another voice – we later ascertained it was the voice of the skipper of the Air Sea Rescue launch that had just picked up a pilot who had ditched in the sea. The voice said, 'What, you again!' This exclamation was explained to the King later in the day. Apparently the pilot who had shouted 'Mayday' and had been picked up by the launch, had twice before in that week been picked up by the same launch. The pilots returned to the station later in the day and described their experiences to the King, who was tremendously interested. It was certainly very thrilling and made me feel very proud that the country had such fine men defending it. Biggin Hill had been heavily bombed just prior to our visit, but it was surprising how quickly the station had been put in order once again.

We continued to visit London almost every day and the King made his regular visits to the embassy, where he met members of his government and sometimes important members of the Allies. On one particular occasion, he had an audience with General de Gaulle. He was a fine tall man, looking very taciturn, but just as I imagined him to be.

8

Royal Occasions

The King and Queen had now commenced to reside at Buckingham Palace from Monday to Friday every week. They would come up from Windsor early on the Monday and return to the Castle after tea on the following Friday. The two Princesses would travel up almost every day. On several occasions the King would call at the Palace for a chat with the royal couple, and I would wait in the ante-room. It was amusing on some mornings to see the Princesses arrive – they had apparently misbehaved on the way up, and when they entered the Palace and waited for the lift to the royal apartment, they would invariably argue as to who had been the culprit. It was pleasant to see that two royal misses could behave exactly as any other children.

On some of these visits to the Palace, our stay was long enough for me to witness some of the special presentation of decorations to heroes by the King.

On 6 May 1942, we left London by the 10.15 a.m. train for Waverley Station, Edinburgh. On our arrival next morning at 9.10 a.m. we drove immediately to Milburn Towers, the HQ of Norwegian naval officers in Scotland. After breakfast we left for Port Edgar and then drove to Leuchars, Fifeshire, where we visited the air station and inspected special planes used in transporting Norwegians to and from Sweden. Of course they travelled as ordinary passengers, as Sweden was neutral. After the inspection, we were entertained to a glorious lunch in the officers' mess. After lunch we paraded with the King on the front porch of the mess and were officially photographed. I was invited to join the group. I always found the officers most anxious to treat me as a guest; so much so, that I fancy the King spoke of me very often.

After a very hectic day, we returned to Milburn Towers, where we stayed the night, after being entertained to a very nice dinner by the officers. We left early next morning for Waverley Station, where we boarded a train for Darlington.

On arrival at Darlington, we were met by the officer commanding Catterick Air Station. We spent a pleasant time touring the station and saw a flight of Norwegian planes perform a special flight for the King. The siren was sounded and the pilots immediately rushed to their planes, boarded them and were in the air very quickly. They all landed one after another. The landing was marred by a slight mishap of a plane landing just a moment too soon after the leader. No one was hurt and very little damage was done to the plane. We then saw a film show of pictures taken by automatic cameras during a scrap.

In the evening I was invited to join the officers for a special dinner given for the King. A special menu card was printed in Norwegian:

MIDDAG

Tomat Suppe

Flyndre Filet

Gron Asparages

Roast Beef

Blomkal

Stekte poteter

Sherry Soufle

Bringebrae Lup
Kaffe

The only lighting consisted of candles placed in wine bottles. Altogether it was an exciting experience, also amusing. At this period the BBC were running a detective programme on the radio called *Inspector Hornlee*, and the PMC and the OC of the station had decided to refer to me as Inspector Hornlee.

After dinner, when the King was being entertained by the senior officers, I was entertained in the mess. I am afraid my drinking capacity was no match for the other officers, but I was determined not to be found under the table. After what had been a memorable day for me, we left the station in time to catch the midnight train to London from Darlington.

We spent the next day in London and then returned to Foliejon late in the afternoon.

On the 14th, the King visited Westfield College at Kiddepore Road, Hampstead, to inspect a detachment of WRNS. They put on a very smart show and the King was pleased with the turnout.

On 17 May, Norway Day, the King attended a special service held at St Martin-in-the-Fields Church. After the service we all went to the Coliseum to view a special show.

We attended Rotherhithe Church on 24 May and afterwards went to The Coppings to spend a few hours with the Duke and Duchess of Kent. The Prince and Princess were sliding down the stair rails when we arrived.

The next week was spent in visiting London and performing the usual duties. During the weekends, the King would spend a deal of time reading the papers and keeping in touch with Norwegian affairs. In the afternoons about 3.00 p.m. I would meet him at the front of the house and we would take a walk round the park. We usually chatted about events of the past few days and the King would inform me of future events and invite me to obtain the necessary details from his colonel. Sometimes he would ask me to call at his study to pick up papers he wished destroyed. On one occasion I slipped up over the time and before I realized it, the King was knocking on my door asking me if I was ready. I made the necessary apologies, but the King merely laughed and said perhaps his watch was fast. On this particular afternoon, he discussed my family affairs and suggested that I invite my wife to join me at the house whenever she needed to get away for a rest. He arranged for another bed to be fitted in my room. He was indeed a most considerate man.

On 2 June, we left Euston for Chester, where we were driven to Thornton Manor, the home of Lord Leverhulme. I was fixed up with a delightful room in the house and while the King was being entertained by his host and hostess, I was having a nice time with other members of the staff. Part of the house was being used as a hospital for convalescents and some of the maids were part-time assistants in the hospital.

We toured the factory at Port Sunlight on the 3rd and then a reception was held for the King in the Assembly Hall. I was making arrangements for my lunch when I was called to attend the main lunch. I found myself seated between two dear old ladies, who appeared immensely interested in what I might be able to tell them about the King. It was a very nice lunch and I thoroughly enjoyed every minute of it. We stayed the night at Thornton Manor, and returned to London early the next day.

On 12 June, the King was invited to attend the Norwegian Home Guard dinner at the Wheatsheaf Hotel, Virginia Water. I was again invited to take a meal with the assembly and was highly amused at the jokes made by the King. He could indeed be amusing at times.

On the 14th we visited Buckingham Palace and the King took lunch with the King and Queen.

We visited the home of the newly appointed Norwegian Minister, a Mr Collier, on the 16th. It was a delightful house called Rawlings at Seer Green in Buckinghamshire.

On 19 June, we left King's Cross at 9.15 p.m. for Edinburgh, where we arrived at 8.20 a.m. next morning. After having breakfast at the Caledonian Hotel, we left for Port Edgar and Milburn Towers and the Command Headquarters.

The King attended the service at the Seamen's Church at Leith on the 21st, then later in the afternoon he visited Craiglochart Hospital to visit some Norwegians there.

We left Edinburgh for Inverness on the 22nd. We were met by the GOC Scottish Command, General Sir Andrew Thorne. We drove in the General's car to Beauly and on to Brahan Castle and Dingwall. Our headquarters for the next few days was to be Brahan Castle.

I discovered the castle to be very old and reputed to be haunted by a charming ghost in the form of a lady who had been deserted by her husband many years before. We none of us had the pleasure of seeing the dear lady, but the King was amused with the story, still more so when he discovered that Commander Smith was occupying the haunted apartment.

We had a delightful dinner of locally caught salmon and then spent the rest of the evening chatting with the officers. On the next day we attended manoeuvres with the troops at Coul House, went on to Strathpeffer and Evanton and then returned to Brahan Castle for dinner in the evening.

In the early morning, I was invited to go salmon fishing with one of the officers and was delighted to be able to gaff a fine specimen. Later we left for Nigg Camp, went on to Mansfield House and Tain and then to Dingwall, returning to Brahan Castle for dinner.

On the 25th we travelled to Evanton to take part in the local manoeuvres at Loch Glass. We had a picnic lunch and watched the events through binoculars loaned from the General. After a pleasant day, we returned to Brahan Castle. In the evening the King was the guest of Sir John Aird for dinner, and we drove out to a pleasant hotel on Loch Garve. Sir John had arranged for me to be served with an excellent dinner and he had also fixed up dinner for his driver. He was a very nice gentleman.

The 26th we drove out to Dornoch, where the railway hotel was being used as a military headquarters. We saw the local contingent of Norwegians perform various evolutions for the King and then returned to Brahan Castle.

We left Brahan Castle early on the 27th for Knoclespool House, Clatt, Aberdeenshire. The hostess was reputed to be a cousin of Mr Roosevelt and was the wife of a British naval commander. I was amused at the way the lady was preserving her special port for the honoured guest only. During the dinner there was apparently a slight misunderstanding over this, and later the King referred to it in a jocular way. I was feeling a little out of things, until the King saw my predicament and at once got the conversation round to include me. He made some comment that he would be lost without his shadow. This of course put me in the picture and from then on I was included in the general conversation. We left Clatt in time to catch the 6.05 p.m. train from Aberdeen for London, where we arrived early next morning. The King stayed in London all day and returned to Foliejon in the afternoon.

On 2 July we visited the Roof Garden of Derry and Toms. It was very interesting. The usual programme of visits to London took place almost every day until the 12th, when we again visited Badminton.

The King took tea on the 15th with Lady Houston Boswell, who lived in a small house just outside of Foliejon Park.

He was the guest, on the 26th, of Colonel Pederson at Deepcut, St George's Hill, Weybridge. On the 28th he visited Mr Hindahl, a member of the Norwegian Government residing at Virginia Water. Next day we left for High Wycombe and then went by train to Leamington and by car to Coventry. A group photograph including the King and Lord Nuffield and other members of the party was taken just outside the main office.

While in the district, we stayed at the Queens Hotel, Birmingham. A dinner was given by Lord Nuffield in the evening. We all retired at 11.00 p.m. and shortly afterwards the air raid siren was sounded. The management had asked me to get the King to the shelter. I managed to persuade him to go to the shelter, which we discovered was an underground part of the hotel through which the hot water pipes ran. The King said during the height of the raid, in which a large number of bombs were dropped in the vicinity, 'I certainly don't relish the idea of being boiled alive.'

We emerged unscathed from the shelter in the early hours of the morning and then went on to inspect the Wolseley Motor Works. On the way we passed the scene of the recent bombing raid and the King was appalled at the damage, which appeared to be in the main to working-class houses.

We left later on 30 July for Reading. On our arrival at Foliejon, we were met by Princess Martha of Norway. She had come over from the USA to spend the birthday anniversary of the King. She was a most delightful woman and immediately captured the hearts of everyone.

We went to Rotherhithe Church on 2 August. The Princess and Prince Olaf accompanied the King. On 3 August, the King's birthday, a special march past of Norwegians had been arranged to take place in Hyde Park. A tent had been erected opposite the Albert Hall and on the instructions of the AOC, I thoroughly examined the area before the King took his stand there. It was quite a memorable occasion to see representatives of all sections of the Norwegians marching past the saluting dais. The whole proceedings were under the control of Admiral Rissar Larsen – a world-famous Norwegian airman. He had flown over the Pole and was at this time a very enthusiastic supporter of the King.

After the march past, we all attended a special ceremony at the Albert Hall and the King had a special dinner provided at the embassy. (I made one of my very infrequent visits home in the evening.)

We attended the christening of Prince Michael of Kent at

Windsor Castle on 4 August. It was quite an occasion.

We went to Badminton on 9 August, and while in London on the 11th, the King visited the Odeon Cinema at Leicester Square. (I forget the name of the picture.) On the 14th we walked through Hyde Park – quite a change, but it was a very nice day. On the 16th, we again visited The Coppings and on the 18th the King visited the Cottage at Taplow, the residence of an old acquaintance of the Norwegian Royal Family. On the 19th, we visited The Herriots, Stanmore Common, where the King lunched with the President of Poland. On the 22nd, the King attended Nortra Ships sports meeting at Shrubbs Hill, Virginia Water.

On 25 August, we heard news of the tragic death of the Duke of Kent. As a leading air force officer, he made routine visits to stations both abroad and within the British Isles. He was, according to the opinion of King Haakon, a family man who loved to be home with his wife and children as often as possible and preferably at weekends. On this occasion he was due to make a routine visit to Iceland, but the trip had to be postponed due to bad weather conditions. He was impatient to fulfil his mission and, as a consequence, set off on a day that was not ideal for flying. Soon after leaving his base at Invergordon, the plane ran into low cloud and crashed into a mountainside. His body was brought back to Windsor and the funeral was held there on 29 August. It was a most impressive ceremony and the members of the Royal Family present were obviously very grieved, especially the Duchess of Kent.

Apart from the usual almost daily visits to London for the next few days, the King had no special engagements. He was frequently accompanied at this time by the Crown Princess Martha.

On 4 September, we attended a special film showing at the Gaumont Studios in Wardour Street. The various pictures taken of the activities of the Crown Princess and the Norwegian royal children, both in Canada and the States, had been made into a film, and the King was invited to see the result. In the film we saw quite a lot of shots of the activity of the Norwegian Air Force, who were at that time training in Canada at a place called Little Norway.

A special demonstration by merchant seamen at the Albert Hall was attended by the King on 12 September.

On 15 September, we motored out to Cambridge University and saw experiments being made with dehydrated foods. Later the King had lunch in College Hall of the university. I was invited to take lunch with the others. On the way to the main hall we passed through a hall containing shields of the various crests of the British Knighthood. It was certainly an interesting visit.

On the 16th the King visited Lord Wigram, a retired Controller of Buckingham Palace who was living in an apartment at Windsor Castle. While the King was being entertained by this gentleman, I was entertained by the staff at Windsor Castle.

On the 27th, we again visited Badminton and the King went into the park adjoining the manor and saw some of the handiwork of Queen Mary. She had, together with helpers, collected a large amount of the timber from the park and placed it out for drying before being used as a fuel on the estate. She used the saw quite as well as her helpers.

We visited Selsdon on 4 October, and after lunch at the Selsdon Hotel, the King attended a demonstration of the ATC from Purley.

The 7th found us again at The Coppings. The Prince (now Duke of Kent) and the Princess (Princess Alexandra) had grown considerably, but were still able to enjoy themselves by sliding down the banister rails.

During the whole of October, we visited London almost every day and the King frequently entertained some young hero or heroine from Norway. He would have an audience with these people and then invite them to take lunch with him. The King used to relate to me their various stories while we were walking in the grounds of the house at weekends.

Some of them had escaped from Nazi tyranny by clever tricks, and some were airmen who had crashed and returned to England by the underground route. Most Norwegians could speak German and this was a great asset in some of their escapes. One of these flyers had crashed in Belgium and managed to return to England via Gibraltar. He was of course assisted by the French underground, but during the journey through Paris, he was ably assisted by a German officer, who of course had no idea as to the Norwegian's proper identity.

Another interesting case was the escape of a Norwegian member of the Storting (the name given to the Norwegian Government). He had been captured by the Germans and was at the time of his escape in an Oslo hospital suffering from ill treatment meted out to him by his captors. His escape was manoeuvred by members of the Norwegian underground. They arrived at the hospital armed with false papers purporting to come from German High Command. Their ruse worked and by the time the Germans had discovered the hoax, the escapee was in Sweden and within a few hours was on his way to England.

On 29 October, we left King's Cross at 10.15 p.m. for Edinburgh. We breakfasted at the North British Hotel and then visited the City Chambers. After inspecting members of the local ARP and witnessing a display at Coupar Street and St Andrews House, we returned to the City Hall, where the King was entertained to lunch by the Lord Provost, Lord Darling. It was impressive to witness the haggis being escorted in by pipers, but the huge amount of whisky they usually drank with one gulp always astounded me.

The next day we visited the Scottish National War Memorial, which stands on a hill overlooking Princes Street. Indeed a majestic place! The inside of the memorial hall houses huge books containing the names of the Scottish dead from the Great War.

Afterwards the King visited Norway House, Leith, and took tea with the principals. On 1 November we attended divine service at the Norwegian Seamen's Church at Leith, and later we visited the Norwegian Gunnery School at Dumbarton, returning to Edinburgh later in the day.

On 2 November, we left by car for Drumtochty Castle, Kincardineshire. On the journey we passed the entrance to Glamis Castle, the birthplace of the Queen of England. Drumtochty was a quaint place in a valley. The Norwegian young people had been moved from Glasgow to this village because the damp air of Glasgow was playing havoc with their health. We returned from Drumtochty by car to Dubton Junction, where we boarded a train for Glasgow. After dinner at the Central Hotel, we left for London, where we arrived next day at 9.15 a.m., then after visiting the embassy, the King returned to Winkfield.

We visited Badminton again on 22 November.

Later in the month, we went to Kingston and the King inspected the sea cadets on the *Steadfast*, then had lunch with local VIPs at Bentalls, a large store in Kingston. The rest of the year was taken up with many visits to London, but nothing very exciting took place.

On 1 January 1943, we attended a Grand Pageant at the Albert Hall; a very impressive ceremony at which many important people were in attendance, including Mr Churchill and the King of England.

On the 6th we stayed in London all night, so I took the opportunity of making a visit home.

We left London on the 15th for Glasgow and on our arrival next day, the King visited the navy at Nelson Street Docks. We drove through the city and were entertained to lunch by the Lord Provost at the City Hall. After lunch the King opened the new Seamen's Club. We left for London at 9.30 p.m. and then attended the Norwegian Church at Rotherhithe.

A member of the Royal Family at Englemere, Ascot Hill, was visited by the King on 6 February. On the 7th we went to Badminton. On 23 February, the King attended a concert organized by the Norwegians at St Martin-in-the-Fields.

On the 27th we went to Wembley Stadium to see an international match. The King of England was present, so was General Montgomery. Another visit to The Coppings was made on 14 March, in order for the King to take tea with the Duchess of Kent. On the 16th we visited regional headquarters, then went to Kingston Barracks and then to Sandown Racecourse. No, there was no race meeting, the course was being used as a special training ground.

The Albert Hall was visited on the 27th, where a special concert was given in aid of the China Relief Fund. We left London later for Barrow-in-Furness and stayed at Abbey House, the home of Sir Charles Craven, the boss of Vickers Armstrong, on 28 March. We later went to the shipyard where the King launched a new Norwegian submarine. I was surprised at the tremendous amount of machinery that could be placed in the submarine.

After the launching, we took a short surface trip and it was very thrilling, but I had no wish to become a member of the crew. The King was entertained by Sir Charles and I was made most comfortable. Sir Charles was truly a sport, but I discovered he was at one time a naval commander, so his hospitality was explained.

We left Furness Abbey at 9.19 a.m. on 29 March for Euston, then after making a few calls in London, we returned to Winkfield. On 9 April, we again visited St Martin-in-the-Fields. On 15 April the King visited Drapers Hall, Frogmorton Street, City of London, where he was entertained by the Worshipful Master of the Hall.

On 26 April, we attended the International Allied Services match at Stamford Bridge, Chelsea's ground. As we were leaving the ground, I ran into my brother Arthur, his wife and son Jimmy. Daisy was so pleased to see me, that she shouted 'Hi! Bert.' The King laughed, and when I later explained that the people were my relatives, he said, 'You could have said a little more to them!'

We went to the headquarters of Fighter Command at Bentley Priory, Stanmore on 5 May. We were shown around the station and saw the 'Ops' room working. I was always thrilled with these visits and the various activities we were able to see. On 6 May, we went to the Chapel Royal, but I forget why. On the 8th we left by car for Barnwell Manor, the home of the Duke of Gloucester. I saw the young Prince

William, who was being taken for a walk by his nurse. On the 9th we attended service at the very quaint old English village church. The King, accompanied by the Duke and Duchess, walked across the fields to the church. We left next day for London.

On 17 May (Norway's Day), the King attended a special service at St Paul's Cathedral, then later we went to the Albert Hall for another ceremony in connection with this special day.

Manchester College, Oxford, was visited on the 18th, and later Hartford College and Bodleian Library. We saw special maps being prepared from holiday snaps which had been submitted to the government. All the workers were girls who appeared to be very adept at their work. On the 30th we visited Windsor Castle, where the King took tea with the King and Queen.

On 4 June we visited Harrow School. The King inspected the school and then attended a concert given by the boys in the Concert Hall, an ancient place where many prominent old pupils had performed in the past, not the least important of whom was Mr Churchill. While the King was being entertained by the Headmaster, I was being entertained in the school tuck shop.

The King visited Hampton Court on 9 June, in connection with a gathering of the Lest We Forget Association.

On the 13th we visited the Norwegian Church at Rotherhithe. While the King was taking coffee with the pastor, Per and I were entertained by the canteen lady. The King had finished his chat with the pastor before Per could finish his coffee. He turned to me and said, 'Did you get your coffee?' I replied that I had succeeded in finishing mine, but Per had not. The King immediately replied, 'Finish your coffee – I'm in no hurry.' We then left for the Albert Hall.

We visited North Weald Air Station on the 19th and made a tour of the station and chatted with some officers. After lunch in the officers' mess, we returned to Foliejon.

On the 27th we visited Wandsworth Town Hall and saw a display by the ATC. On 30 June, we visited Oriel College, Oxford. This visit was in connection with the Prince, who had been educated at Oxford.

On 3 July, the King was invited by Admiral Sir Edward Evans to attend a display at the London Fire Brigade Headquarters. The King enjoyed the daring display put on by the experts.

9

Scotland the Brave

At 7.20 p.m. on the 5th, we left for Brahan Castle, Dingwall. On the 6th we visited gun detachments at Fortrose and Cromarty and other Norwegians at Nigg. We stayed the night at Brahan Castle and on the 7th left to attend manoeuvres in the mountains. We left for Rannock Hotel, Kinloch, Rannock, at 3.00 p.m. It was an exciting drive in a car provided by Scottish Command. We arrived in time for dinner. I was invited to attend the dinner with the King, Crown Prince, Commander Smith and General Ritchie, but in view of the talk being mostly business, I excused myself and later dined alone in the main restaurant.

While the King was dining, a piper – an old member of the Black Watch, the General's regiment – entertained the guests with pipe music. He later entered the house and we had lots of fun with other members of the household. The piper was well primed with whisky and before the evening was over, he invited me to try the pipes. I made a terrible noise. Some days later, the King mentioned this noise and laughed heartily when I related the episode to him.

Early next day we breakfasted together at the hotel, then left shortly afterwards for Dall Camp, where the now well trained Norwegian troops were undergoing manoeuvres.

The King inspected the various phases of their training and then we all assembled in the main dining hall for a lunch of good Norwegian fare. The King sat with the Commander and other officers, but other ranks were also present at lunch in the same hall. The King chatted freely as usual to all and sundry.

At 4.30 p.m. we left Dall Camp for a drive across the moors to Aviemore. Here we stayed at Drumitoul Lodge, the headquarters of the Special Service troops. I was allotted a cabin with other officers and then later we sat down to a magnificent dinner, which was attended by many young Norwegians connected with the Norwegian underground soldiers. Most of them had recently returned from raids into enemy-held country. The next day we proceeded to the local mountains and saw demonstrations of the various methods adopted by these gallant men in hampering the enemy in their beloved country. We saw them re-enact some of their choicest expeditions.

I will endeavour to describe some of them, because they thrilled me terrifically at the time; memory gets a bit dim as time passes, but here goes: A young blond Norwegian who had arrived back in Scotland but 24 hours before re-enacted his most recent exploit. It was his task to steal certain papers from a local German HQ. He was entirely alone on this mission. The house being used by the Germans was surrounded by guards, both in the immediate vicinity and at a distance. One young hero arrived on the scene just as the officers were dining. He was armed only with a fisherman's knife, which he carried in his belt. He approached the house very quietly and had soon killed the guard situated in the rear of the house – almost at the same instant as he struck the fatal blow, he was climbing over the roof of the house and very soon he was looking down upon the guard in the front of the house; he waited for the guard to turn, and then leaped upon his back and stifled the guard's attempt at a scream, and in a few seconds the guard was lying dead. He quickly dragged the body to the nearby bushes and rapidly put on the German's uniform. He then entered the house and was soon ransacking a set of drawers. Shortly after, he emerged from the house with the documents he had set out to capture.

Later we saw another drama re-enacted by more young

Norwegians who had returned to Scotland to report the result of their mission. Their particular mission was dropping machine-gun parts, and then dropping themselves in the vicinity in order to instruct the recipients in the assembly and working of the gun.

The drops had been successful and all the parties were busy with the instructing, when a sudden raid was made on the hut which they were using by a German raiding party who had been informed by a 'Quisling'. Some of the party of young Norwegians dived headlong through the closed window and had disappeared out of sight before the first German entered the hut; the remainder were closely and brutally examined by the Germans, but it appeared that they had been unsuccessful in hiding the parts of the gun. Unfortunately, one of the searchers saw a tiny spring lodged in the corner. On picking it up, he recognized it as a vital part of a gun and immediately ordered the arrest of the occupants of the hut. He had hardly uttered the command when the would-be prisoners suddenly overwhelmed the Germans, and after strangling them followed their comrades through the window.

Of course all the actors in this re-enaction were young Norwegians who had taken part in actual raids of such a nature and none of the actors were injured, but I still wonder how these men who dived through the glass of the closed window managed to get off with hardly a scratch. Most of these lads were barely out of their teens, and what is more they were very nice-looking boys, but boys who hated anyone who desired to hurt Norway.

After the demonstration, we left by car for Banff, where we stayed at the Fife Arms Hotel. This was a delightful place, situated on the edge of the harbour wall.

Early next morning, we left for Buckie, which was the temporary home of many Norwegian fishermen who were at that time plying their calling in the local seas. We toured the local docks and the King spoke to some Danish fishermen who had just been brought in for questioning by the naval authorities. They at first appeared to be very distressed, but

Per and myself
outside Norway House,
London

Norwegian Navy personnel before taking over of torpedo destroyers

King Haakon of Norway, Lord Harewood and Mayor of Sheffield on their way to inspect Sheffield steel works

H.M. King Haakon VII visiting headquarters of the USA navy personnel. Myself in background

Friendly conversation with a little Norwegian Miss

Visiting with Norwegian fishermen – Buckie

Oxford University – RNVR

ng Haakon VII, Crown Prince Olav and myself leaving for a memorial service at St
ul's Cathedral, London, in honour of United States President Franklin Delano
osevelt

Carbisdale Castle – Scotland

Drumlanrig Castle (Home of the Duke of Buccleuch)

Places visited by King Haakon VII accompanied by his shadow

King Haakon of Norway leaving the Norwegian Embassy for Buckingham Palace

Marriage of Stephanie Doreen Coates to William Flett Forman, 4 March 1944

Son Arthur Albert   Daughter Stephanie Doree

after a chat with the King in their own language, they became very cheerful once again.

The King held an audience which was attended by some of the local Norwegian dignitaries and later we all proceeded to the Strathlene Hotel on the front, where we had a gorgeous lunch. After the lunch the King invited everyone present, including the waitresses, to join the group that was to be photographed in the front of the hotel. I still have the photo, which shows the King, together with all the invited guests and the local Chief of police.

We left the hotel at 3.30 p.m. by car for Aberdeen, and left the Granite City on the 5.45 p.m. train to London, where we arrived early next day. After making the usual calls in London, the King returned to Foliejon later in the day. The next three days were spent in London.

On 15 July 1943, we boarded the train at Slough and travelled to Cardiff, where we were met by the Lord Mayor. We then travelled to the docks to inspect a Norwegian freighter that had managed to elude the German raiders for a record time. We all later returned to Cardiff and enjoyed a magnificent lunch put on by the city. We returned to Slough later in the day.

The next week was spent as usual – commuting to and from London.

We left Euston at 1.00 p.m. on 27 July for Chester. A small party, consisting of the King, Colonel Nordlie and Commander Smith, a representative of Lord Leverhulme and myself, travelled in a small coach fitted with a kitchen and we had a glorious feed on the train. We arrived at Thornton Manor later in the day and were met there by Lord Leverhulme, who appeared to me to be a very charming old gentleman but unfortunately suffered with deafness.

On the 28th we left by car for Blundellsands, Liverpool, where the Norwegian Navy had a small radar school. After inspecting the staff, we went to visit the Allied Council at Liverpool. On the return journey, we stopped at Birkenhead and were entertained to sherry by the Mayor and councillors. The King dined with the Leverhulmes and I was entertained by the Leverhulmes' secretary, who knew several Special Branch colleagues of mine.

We left Thornton Manor next day and boarded the 9.30 a.m. train from Chester to London, and later went to Foliejon.

On 1 August, we again visited Queen Mary at Badminton; then followed the usual routine in London, with the exception that the King visited the Middlesex Hospital on the 6th, when he saw some Norwegian patients.

On 12 August, the King visited Culham Manor, Oxfordshire, the home of Sir Esmond Ovey, a retired ambassador. It was a delightful old house, modernized in parts. While the King was being entertained by Sir Esmond, Per and I were being taken on a tour of the grounds by a member of the household, who also gave us a brief history of the place. Altogether a very interesting afternoon. On the 21st the King again visited Scrubbs Hill, the headquarters of the Nortra Ships Sports Club. Later we drove to Warfield House, the home of Sir Thomas Sopwith, where the King was entertained to dinner. We watched a display by the London ARP at Wembley Stadium on 22 August.

On 24 August, we left King's Cross at 1.10 p.m. for Leeds and then went to Harewood House, the residence of the Princess Royal and Lord Harewood. We were met by the Princess Royal. It was usual for me to stay at the same place as the King, but on this occasion I was unable to get accommodation at Harewood House because part of the house was being utilized as a convalescent hospital, so I was instructed to stay at the Harewood Hotel just outside the gate of the Harewood estate. It was owned by the Princess Royal. Before leaving, the King informed me that he would not be leaving the house until next morning.

On the 25th, the King, dressed in the uniform of a British Army Colonel – he was the Honorary Colonel of the Yorkshire Regiment of the Green Howards – left in the Princess Royal's car driven by her chauffeur and accompanied by me, for Richmond, Yorkshire.

The King inspected the troops and then was entertained by the Commander to lunch. During the tour of the barracks, the King was entertained by the members of the WO's and sergeants' mess, and took a drink from the loving cup. He was always sporting enough to agree to most suggestions. We returned to London later in the day.

On 9 September, the King lunched with the Polish President at The Herriots, Stanmore. Practically the whole of September was spent commuting between Foliejon and London. Our visits during this period included the London Pavilion.

We left King's Cross on 7 October for Edinburgh, where we stayed at the North British Hotel. The King on this occasion was the guest of the GOC Scottish Command, and the main interest of the visit was the inspection of the troops at Glencorse Barracks.

A surprise visit to Craiglochart Hospital was paid by the King on the 9th; this hospital was on the outskirts of Edinburgh, and he later attended a concert at the Usher Hall.

On the 10th he attended divine service at the Norwegian Church at Leith. On the 11th we went to Port Edgar and Milburn Towers and Corsterphine for various inspections. We left Waverley Station at 9.45 p.m. for King's Cross, where we arrived at 8.30 a.m. next day. After a stay in London, we returned to Foliejon later in the afternoon.

The next fortnight the usual programme was adopted until on the 24th we went to Oxford and attended a concert at the Sheldonian Theatre. It was a very quaint place and obviously very old.

London saw us daily for the next few weeks and on 12 November we left King's Cross at 3.50 p.m. for Newcastle, where we arrived at 10.15 p.m. We stayed at the Central Hotel, and as the hotel could be entered from the station, we were soon under cover.

I was pleased to find that the manager of the hotel was an old colleague of mine who had been a member of the Branch until he was seriously injured by enemy action during a raid on London.

On the 13th we left to tour the docks at North Shields. The King spoke to several Norwegian seamen on a tanker that was undergoing repairs after damage in the Atlantic. We then returned to Newcastle and the King was entertained to lunch at the Mansion House, then we went to the Laing Art Gallery and later to the Norwegian Hotel, Osborne Road, Jesmond, and in the evening to the Norwegian Club in Northumberland Street.

We went to the Seamen's Church on the 14th in North Shields, returning later to the Central Hotel. We left at 2.12 p.m. for King's Cross, arriving at 9.20 p.m. The King decided to stay in London for the night, so when he was safely bedded down, I made one of my visits home.

Our travelling was confined to London and Foliejon until 28 November, when we made another visit to Queen Mary at Badminton.

About this time, Per had been expressing the desire to get back to sea and he was relieved from his job and posted to the navy training establishment at Liverpool. He subsequently joined the Norwegian Navy at Lerwick and was then engaged servicing the fast boats used for transporting Special Service troops to Norway.

On 3 December, the King was entertained at the Holborn Restaurant, and as a consequence he stayed in London, and I was thus able to pay another flying visit home. We returned to Foliejon next day and spent the next seven weeks travelling to and from London.

Our visits during the Christmas period included lunch at Vintners Hall, Upper Thames Street, a visit to the Kodak factory at Harrow, attendance at divine service at Rotherhithe Seamen's Church and lunch at the Dorchester Hotel. I found it very depressing because Clarice had made arrangements to be at Foliejon for Christmas and I hardly saw her. Such is life!

Commander Smith had been an inmate of the Masonic Hospital for some weeks, suffering from some kind of cancer. He died on 12 January 1944, and the King attended the funeral at Putney on the 17th. The King was very grieved at Commander Smith's death; he was very attached to him. During his sickness, we visited the hospital every day.

On 29 January 1944, we left Waterloo Station for Portsmouth Harbour, where we boarded the *Glaisdale* and after a tour of inspection, we returned to the harbour and then boarded the *Victory*. The King was entertained to lunch by the Admiral's coxswain. I remember the occasion well, because I bumped my head on the beams of Nelson's cabin – they must have been very short men in the old days. We returned to Waterloo at 5.15 p.m. and then went back to Foliejon.

The 11th of February found us at Ealing Film Studios to see shots made of the war epic *The Saving of the Demetrius*. I was delighted to see how the camera was made to show scenes that I thought almost impossible to photograph. I was surprised to see what purported to be the tanker floating helpless in the stormy Atlantic. When I subsequently saw the film, it appeared as if the actual scene had been shot in the Atlantic, the huge waves were so realistic, but the shot was in fact taken of a small model floating in a huge tank, and the supposed waves were created by men operating various gadgets.

About this period, Per was replaced by another young Norwegian, named Raedar Nyborg, a member of the wartime Norwegian Air Force. He was working as a lumberjack in Sweden when the Germans invaded Norway, but like many more of his kind, he soon found a way of reaching Britain. He was a very nice young fellow, perhaps not so intellectual as Per, but nevertheless very friendly and most affable with everyone. During the time I knew him, he was always performing a good deed for someone, and he was quickly accepted as a friend by the locals.

Raedar joined us at the embassy, and on the way home to Foliejon we ran into thick fog. After we had managed to negotiate the streets of Windsor, we found the task of finding our way almost hopeless. I alighted from the car and attempted to lead Raedar by using a torch and walking along the white line, but though we managed to travel a few more miles, I found the task well nigh impossible and decided to enlist the aid of the local police. I rang them up from a public house which was nearby and they were soon on the scene, and with their help we managed to reach Foliejon without any serious trouble.

We never had any serious mishaps with the cars while the young Norwegians were driving. They were excellent drivers and though inclined to drive a little fast at times, they always seemed to have complete control of the situation. By arrangement with the Norwegian authorities, I always mastered the driving of every car we used; though it was not part of my duty to drive – after all, one cannot concentrate on two tasks at one time – the fact remained I was always prepared to drive the car in case of a mishap to the driver, and as we were on the road during heavy bombing raids, accidents were always uppermost in our minds.

About this period, Steve brought her latest admirer down to see me and, in fact, to ask my permission for them to marry. Naturally, both Clarice and I were very disappointed to find that Steve had chosen a future husband who would eventually take her thousands of miles from us. Of course it could not be helped; after all, we all have our own lives to live, and many members of families just as close as ours had been separated in the past. I knew that if we objected, Steve was adamant enough to make up her own mind and we would have lost her just the same, but under circumstances entirely different. We were always devoted to each other and I would rather have died than have her leave the family circle without my blessing.

On 19 February, we again visited Wembley Stadium, this time to see the English and Scottish international football match. Quite a few of the Allied chiefs were present and the King and Queen honoured the crowd with their presence. Of course King Haakon spent the time at the match in the company of the royal couple. I thought at the time that our King looked very ill, but in spite of this he put on a very brave show.

The next day, Sunday, we again visited Badminton. It was

a beautiful day and when the King got in the car, he told me that we could stop to pick up hitch-hikers, if I thought it was OK. Shortly after leaving Reading, we did just that and our first hitch-hiker was a guardsman endeavouring to spend a few hours with his wife at Bristol. As we took him as far as Chippenham, he only had another 20 miles to cover. He sat with the King in the car and I could see by the mirror that they were engaged in conversation the whole time. He had no idea who his benefactor was until I told him when he alighted. His wonderful salute was a just reward.

On the return journey from Badminton, we picked up two members of the WRNS and the King must have kept them highly amused, because they were laughing heartily almost from the time they entered the car. They had apparently recognized the King from the onset, but were afraid to mention this, but on leaving the car just outside Reading, they graciously bowed and thanked the King for his kindness.

We visited the *Times* office in London on the 24th.

For the next two months, we travelled almost daily to London, but sometimes merely walked through the home park. I usually met the King at the front of the house and we would then walk around the grounds. On one of these occasions, I was a bit late in leaving my room. Just as I was about to leave, I heard a knock on my door and was a little shocked to find the King waiting there. I apologized, but the King merely shrugged his shoulders and said, 'I'm a bit early.'

During this period, on 3 March to be exact, I obtained a couple of days off, in order to be present at Steve's wedding. I had already approached the King with a view to getting a relief, but he didn't like the idea of a stranger, so he arranged to remain in the vicinity of the house until I returned.

On the 4th, the day of the wedding, we were all busy. Arrangements had been made to hold the wedding feast at a hall situated near the house, but during the night it was damaged by an enemy bomb so we had to make other arrangements. We decided in the end to use the large private bar at the local pub, which was appropriately called We Anchor In Hope.

The arrangements for the wedding had been made by Bill – my future son-in-law – and the rest of the family. My dear mother had fixed the making of the cake – made with ersatz materials, but we were lucky to have such a thing during the war. Drinks were obtained in sufficient quantities to satisfy all concerned.

The arrival of the time for Steve and me to leave for the church made me feel both proud and sad. I was proud to be able to lead my daughter to the altar, but sad to think that it meant losing her for good.

The happy couple left the gathering, which had been quite a success, at the pub, and they left the house some time later for London, where they boarded the train for Peterhead, Scotland.

The best man, Cecil, accompanied them to King's Cross, but during the last few minutes before the train was due to leave, he sat in the train and was so engrossed in conversation that he did not notice it was leaving; as a consequence he was forced to be an unwilling passenger on the train until it arrived at Peterborough, about 200 miles away.

I remained at home until Sunday afternoon, when I returned to Foliejon, where I was pleased to find everything OK. The King travelled to London on Monday, and during the afternoon when we were walking through the park, he asked me how the wedding went.

The King visited St Martin-in-the-Fields on 9 April, and later went to the Coliseum to see a show put on in aid of charity.

On the 21st, we drove to Windsor Castle, where the King took tea with the Royal Family – the occasion being Princess Elizabeth's birthday.

On 30 April, we went by train to Avonmouth via Bristol. We were accompanied on the journey by the Norwegian Government and the Ambassador.

When I travelled with the King on these journeys, liquid

refreshment was provided for everyone, including myself. The King seldom took any strong drink – just an occasional glass of sherry. My seat companion on this particular journey was the Ambassador, a very charming man, but apt to be cross with anyone taking strong drink. In view of the special circumstances and in order not to upset the feelings of the Ambassador, I made arrangements for the steward to bring me gin with water. This little deception proved very useful and no one was annoyed.

The object of this journey to Avonmouth was to enable the Norwegian Government to thank the skipper of a Norwegian vessel for his courage in bringing large quantities of goods and oil to this country, without the single loss of one member of the crew from enemy action. The King presented a medal to the radio operator, who was in fact the wife of the first officer. She was a Canadian girl who had married the officer during the war. The vessel on this occasion was laden with fuel oil and the decks were covered with aeroplanes. A very valuable cargo.

I forget how many times this vessel had crossed the Atlantic without ever being attacked by the enemy, but I know it was a fine achievement. After the ceremony of presenting the medal, we were all entertained lavishly by the skipper. On my departure I was laden with cigarettes and tobacco; in fact, I was thrilled at the way I was treated – just as if I was a hero. Of course these wonderful sailors adored their King and looked upon me as something special because I was his 'shadow'. I can assure you, by this time I had learned to admire the King and would have championed him anywhere.

On 2 May, the King visited the Duke of York Theatre, St Martin's Lane. I forget what show was on – it was usually a charity performance of some kind.

Electra House was visited on the 10th and on 1 June the King was invited to tour the Prisoners of War's Exhibition being held at Clarence House. This was later the residence of Queen Mary.

On the odd afternoon when we did not go to London, the

King would take the lady of the house and her companion to visit one of the cinemas in Windsor. He would give me the money to purchase the tickets and we would all wait in the entrance until the driver had returned from parking the car and then we would all sit together to watch the show.

10

Manoeuvres

On 2 June, the King called me to his study and outlined a trip he intended to make on the morrow. It entailed a cross-country journey – difficult in those days because of the absence of road signs, earlier removed so that the enemy would be confused. I used to study the route and where any difficulty might arise, I would ask the local police to assist me in a discreet manner. Usually their assistance would be a motorcyclist, who would recognize the car and lead us to a pre-arranged point. On this occasion, the visit was to the house of Mr Law, a government minister, who was intending to outline the most important occurrence to happen in a few days' time – viz. the great events of D-Day. We arrived at the house at the stated time, and as the King had decided to remain at home for the rest of the evening, Raedar and I strolled into the village of Buxted, but nothing of the future events could be gleaned from the locals. It was obviously a well-kept secret.

The next day, we went by car for a trip to Brighton and along the coast to Newhaven. The front was deserted except for soldiers and other servicemen. The surrounding countryside was one mass of armament – there were huge tanks and other implements of war and the neighbouring sea was covered with crafts of all kinds. I noticed hundreds of landing craft, similar to those I had seen on a previous expedition to Portsmouth. They were queer-looking vessels, but capable of holding large numbers of men and armaments. Some of the vessels were armed with electrically fired guns; I subsequently saw some of these vessels in action during manoeuvres on Loch Fyne in Scotland. There was lots of activity, but not a civilian to be seen anywhere. It was obvious to us all that great things were about to be started. There was great secrecy everywhere, so we were left to make our own conjectures as to what was about to happen.

We stayed at Buxted during the following night and the sky was full of aeroplanes making constant trips to enemy country. Now and again an inquisitive German plane would be heard in the sky and the occasional bomb exploding in the distance.

We travelled to London on 5 June and then returned to Foliejon.

The 6th was a very eventful day; the news had come that our forces had landed in France and everything was going successfully. We travelled to London daily and the King made several broadcasts to Norway, and on 14 June he visited the Union Jack Club in Waterloo Bridge Road. The raids by the enemy bombers and the frequent dropping of V1s made our journeys a little more hazardous. The King would continue on his journey in spite of the sounding of the warning siren. Many times bombs dropped much too close to be comfortable, but still we carried on.

On 18 June, we again went to Badminton and the Dowager Queen Mary actually smiled at me for a change. She used to look at me always with a severe regard, but apparently the good news from France had had its effect on all and sundry.

The King toured a series of aircraft factories at Kingston and Thames Ditton on 21 June. We all lunched at the Crown Hotel, then travelled to London. London saw us daily for the next week or so.

On 2 July, the King visited Lord Southesk at Sunningdale. On 11 July, the King left Euston for Glasgow, where we arrived at 7.10 a.m. next morning.

We had breakfast at St Enochs Hotel and then left in a

Scottish Command car for Stirling and then on to Callander, where the King inspected Norwegian transport that had been especially trained for fighting in mountainous country.

After leaving Callander we travelled through the beautiful Trossachs to Ardlui, where we lunched at a lovely spot on the famous Loch Lomond shores.

After lunch we travelled to Inverary in Argyllshire. We arrived at the Admiral's house at 4.00 p.m. The King visited the Duke of Argyll – a queer old chap with a strange voice and stranger ideas about modern humanity.

On the 13th, we went on manoeuvres with a large force of navy and army men. The first episode was a mock landing. We boarded a small tank landing craft and followed the main body to the seat of the landing. The foremost craft were fitted with electrically controlled guns; when they fired, the noise was terrific and their shells burst simultaneously on the shore – it was as if the earth was swept with a terrific flash of lightning. Larger guns fired on the nearby countryside and, soon after, men were rushing ashore; in their immediate rear, large tanks were landed and were seen engaging with the imaginary enemy.

The whole scene was very realistic and more so when it was realized that live ammunition was being used. The whole operation impressed me.

Later in the day we landed on the 'taken' country and covered the ground, accompanied by a General. A slight mistiming had occurred and for a few minutes our lives were in jeopardy from nearby machine-guns; we managed to get into a shelter just in time. I was really appalled at the terrible effect of the flame-throwers; I should have hated to have been on the receiving end of those terrible things.

The King made a quick tour of the camp early next day and we all assembled at the Admiral's house for lunch. I was served a very pleasant meal by the WRN PO cook. As she was a bit busy she supplied me with a large tankard of beer to refresh me while I waited for it. She supplied me with another large tankard with my lunch. It was unfortunate that the party left to continue the journey a little earlier than was expected. I am not too good at carrying large quantities of liquid, so nature called me rather urgently at times.

Well, we left on our journey soon after lunch and I was unable to relieve myself of the huge quantities of liquid before we left. I was informed by the driver that it would be almost four hours before we made the first stop, so I settled down to make the most of things, but it was becoming increasingly difficult as we proceeded on our way. After what seemed to me to be an eternity, we arrived at Glencoe.

By this time we were in a very remote part of the country – rocks and still more rocks everywhere the eye could see. I was in agony, so decided to do something about my predicament. The King and the Crown Prince were in the car, separated from the driver and myself with a glass screen. I decided now was the time and turned to the King, who seeing I was urgent about something, instructed the Crown Prince to wind up the dividing window. I then told the King I wanted to relieve myself. He laughed and told the driver to stop the car to enable me to alight. The situation was grim, because we were in a column of 20 cars, one of which was being driven by a woman driver. Modesty was out of the question so far as I was concerned. I alighted and ran for the nearest rock. When I had relieved myself, I discovered that I was not alone – even the lady driver had taken advantage of the stop. Some colonel turned to me and said, 'The fellow that decided on this move deserves a medal.'

On arriving back at the car, I apologized to the King, but he dismissed the whole thing with a grin, and subsequently told me never to hesitate if such a thing occurred again.

After this strange interlude, we carried on through the delightful western country of Scotland, along the banks of Loch Leven to Fort William and Spean Bridge. Here we stopped for tea and chatter. The incident of Glencoe came up and everybody laughed heartily about the whole affair. After tea we travelled on to Kingussie and stayed the night at the Gordon Hotel.

On the 15th, we left for Aviemore, where the King was to be entertained by Special Service troops. We were shown once again how the troops engaged on Special Service hoodwinked the Germans. We remained at the camp until 5.00 p.m. when we left for Perth, arriving there at 7.30 p.m.

We stayed at the Royal George Hotel. The King was entertained to dinner by the officers of Scottish Command; I dined in the same room, but alone. I had the same fare and as a special treat I was served with a bottle of vintage port.

At 9.00 a.m. next day, we left for Broughty Ferry, where the King inspected the 52nd Division, then to Dundee, where he inspected the submarine flotilla and minesweepers. We had lunch at the Commander's residence and then left at 3.00 p.m. on the ferry for Woodhaven, where the King inspected some Catalinas at the local base. Then on to Leuchars.

We stayed in the officers' mess and I had a great time with the station adjutant and the padre, who was a very amusing raconteur.

On the 17th the King inspected various installations and later we saw many Lockheeds and Mosquitoes.

At 11.30 a.m. we went on the moor to watch troops training. At 3.00 p.m. we went to St Andrews and were given accommodation at Montcrieff House, right opposite the St Andrews clubhouse. For dinner we drove to the officers' mess, where the officers entertained the King and the Proctor of the university. I had drinks with Colonel Firby, a very charming host indeed.

The local troops were inspected on the 18th at 10.00 a.m., and then lunch was given by the officers.

We left at 2.00 p.m. for Coupar and later to the residence of General Sir Andrew Thorne, GOC Scottish Command. We had dinner here and I tried my hand with some of the guns and revolvers on the range, not with a lot of success.

We later left for Edinburgh, where we boarded the train for London at 9.40 p.m.

After arriving at King's Cross at 7.10 a.m. the next day, we travelled to the embassy for talks on current topics – the King liked to be acquainted with the latest information regarding the progress of the war and how things were with his countrymen in Norway. Then the King took lunch with Admiral Sir Edward Evans and was joined by Field Marshal Smuts, who was in England at the time to study the progress of the war in Europe. I found the Field Marshal a very fine gentleman, who was quite willing to chat with the rank and file.

During a short discussion with the King while on this visit, a discussion in which I was invited to take part, I had the temerity to ask the Field Marshal for his autograph. I expected to be rebuffed for such forwardness – having decided to make the request in a hurry – but I was pleasantly surprised when he acquiesced. At a later date I met the Field Marshal again when he invited the King to take dinner with him at his hotel.

In the course of the next few weeks, the King made daily visits to London and on occasions remained at the embassy for the night.

On 2 August, after business at the embassy, we visited the headquarters of the Special Service – the people who were operating in enemy territory. Here we met Colonel Wilson, a very pleasant man. I was entertained with refreshments, while the King and the Colonel were discussing the activities of the underground workers in Norway.

On 4 August, the King visited Windsor Castle and had tea with the King and Queen. When he left, Princess Elizabeth came to the door, where they stood for some time laughing and talking. The King always seemed to be a popular visitor when visiting our Royal Family.

We continued our daily visits to London and on 13 August, the King visited Queen Mary at Badminton. He remained here until 4.30 p.m., and as Clarice was at that time staying with her sister at Bristol, Raedar, our driver, decided it would be a good time to pay a quick visit there. We picked up Clarice and Madge, and they returned with us to Chipping Sodbury, where they caught the bus back to

Bristol, and we returned to Badminton.

The following weeks were spent travelling to and from London.

On the 25th, whilst on our usual visit to London, the King visited the Shaftesbury Hotel, where a large number of Norwegians were staying – they were mainly refugees and on this occasion consisted mostly of women and children.

On the 27th, the King visited Queen Wilhelmina of Holland. She was living at that time at a house called The Shrubbery on the outskirts of Maidenhead. She had been on a visit to America to see her daughter, who is now Queen Juliana. I was surprised to see what a motherly woman the Queen was, and though she merely mumbled something to me, she appeared to be a pleasant woman. The King had visited her earlier during his sojourn in England, just after the Queen had been evacuated from Holland.

On the 29th, we went to The Abbey, Ashton Abbots, where the King lunched with President Benes. I had a very interesting talk with some of the President's advisers and felt very sad to think such fine men were forced to live like hunted beasts.

The next few weeks were spent alternately in Winkfield and London. On several occasions when in London, we visited the News Cinema. The King was interested in hearing and seeing the latest news.

A Norwegian exhibition being held at Dorland House was visited by the King on 11 September.

He went to the premiere of a film called *The Return of the Viking* on 12 September.

On the 15th he lunched with King Peter and the Queen of Yugoslavia at the Bucks Club in Piccadilly. This club was badly damaged during the war.

On 20 September, we visited the News Theatre in Leicester Square. We continued our visits to London almost daily, and during these jaunts the King paid several visits to the Shaftesbury Hotel to chat with newcomers. We left Euston Station on 8 October at 8.50 p.m. for Glasgow and arrived at the Central Station at 7.10 a.m. next day. After breakfast at the Central Hotel, we drove by car to Largs in Ayrshire, where the King was to be made a Freeman of the Burgh. I discovered that Largs was almost a Viking town, having been recaptured from the northern Vikings about 600 years before.

We returned to Glasgow in the day and the King then visited the Seamen's Hostel in Vincent Street. He was later entertained to dinner at the Central Hotel by the British Council and I was invited to attend the dinner. I was pleased to meet an old school chum – he was the bandmaster of the military band that was entertaining the guests at the dinner. Of course we had an additional drink together after the others had retired and we chatted with great gusto about the days when we were boys together at Hythe.

On the 10th the King lunched at the City Chambers and I was again invited to partake of some of the fare. I was highly amused to meet one of the curators of the building who had a vivid imagination and could see all sorts of figures in the stones that the walls of the chambers were built of. Apparently I must have been an interested listener, because before I left, he gave me a box of cigars. Truly a gift from the gods in those days.

We later visited the art galleries at Kelvingrove and then attended a concert at St Andrews Hall. We left Central Station for London at 9.30 p.m. that evening. Though we arrived in London at 7.30 a.m., we remained in the city until the late afternoon.

On 14 October, we visited Wembley Stadium to see the match between England and Scotland. The King of England and several notabilities were there, including Field Marshal Lord Montgomery. The visits to London continued and on 20 October, we visited Windsor Castle for the christening of the Duke of Gloucester's son.

On the 25th, the King lunched with the principals of the *Daily Telegraph* at the *Telegraph* office.

During the next few days the King visited the BBC in London to make a broadcast to Norway, visited Badminton

once more, and lunched at the Baltic Exchange.
On 1 November, he lunched with Lord Teviot at his house in London. On the 3rd we again visited Windsor, where the King attended the funeral of Princess Beatrice. On the 4th, we all went to the cinema at Maidenhead – the Rialto. On 16 November, the King visited the West Herts Hospital at Hemel Hempstead.

I had a day off on 18 November, being relieved by Dickinson. I left home at 7.30 p.m. to catch the train, and while waiting for my train, I saw a terrific cloud of smoke suddenly shoot up into the air in the direction of our house, but did not realize at the time that a V2 had exploded at the bottom of our road. I continued on my journey to Windsor.
Early on 20 November, I received a telephone call from Steve to say that the house had been badly damaged by the explosion of a V2. I told the King and he arranged for me to visit home as soon as we arrived in London.
On my arrival at home, I discovered a tremendous amount of damage, but fortunately no member of our family had been injured; the house was a shambles. The family had been sitting in the front room when the rocket hit the house at the bottom of the road – the front door was upstairs and the roof had completely disappeared. Bill had gone down to assist the injured and Clarice, together with Steve, remained at the house that night. When we had tidied up a bit, we decided that Clarice should return with me and Bill made arrangements to take Steve to his relatives in Aberdeen.
On 22 November, we stayed in London – the King at the embassy and I stayed at the Yard, where a colleague fixed up a bed for me. Later in the day, while the King was engaged with urgent business at the embassy, I returned to have a look at our house and stayed the night. I returned early in the morning and then accompanied the King to Portsmouth.
He visited the Norwegian destroyer the *Stord*, lying at

anchor offshore, and we had lunch in the wardroom. We later visited the *Victory* in Portsmouth Dockyard and returned to London at 5.02 p.m., then drove to Winkfield.

On 24 November, we visited the Danish Exhibition at Old Bond Street. On 5 December, during our usual visit to London, the King lunched at the Tallow Chandlers Hall in the City.

On 6 December, the King went to the Royal Academy and later to University Hospital, Gower Street. We continued the daily trips to London with the odd visit to some special person.

We visited the Royal Albert Docks on 18 December, and the King took lunch with the captain of a Norwegian vessel. I forget the name just now, but this captain was a friend of mine and his chief steward was always most generous. (This same man visited Vancouver after the war and in my absence entertained Bill and Steve with friends. We were down in California at the time, but even so I discovered a bottle waiting for me when we returned from our holiday.)

On Christmas Day the King visited the Norwegian Seamen's Church at Rotherhithe and, after lunching at a London hotel, we returned to Foliejon.

In the evening we had a party at the house – Raedar, Per and Bill were there, together with Clarice. We had plenty of aquavit and as a consequence everyone was very matey at the end. Poor Bill had to be on duty at Lincoln's Inn Fields on Boxing Day – this meant an early start. Raedar had arranged to take him to Windsor Station, but we had a job to awaken him.

Eventually all was well and Bill caught his train, but unfortunately he was nearly brought back to Windsor. He had fallen asleep and was only awakened in time to get off the train before it gathered speed. He was very glad to return home after duty that day. It was a grand party and toasts were drunk to absent friends. Steve was up in the Highlands and we poor misguided chumps were in the lowlands, but not feeling all that low.

We continued to visit London for the next few weeks, and as things were going fairly well with the war, I decided to have a day off and was relieved by Dickinson.

It was not much fun at home, because Arthur was away and Steve was up in Scotland and Bill was expecting to be repatriated to Canada at any date. The little time off was, however, a respite from the continuous day-to-day vigil.

11

The End at Last

London saw the King very often during the next few weeks, but he again visited Prince George of Greece at Great Fosters on 13 January, when they lunched together.

On 23 January, we left London at 1.10 p.m. from King's Cross for Leeds. By this time meals were not served on trains, so we took a picnic lunch with us. It was rather pleasant having an informal meal with the King and his ADC. I remember we had chicken and other food topped up with a bottle of good beer. The King amused both the Colonel and myself with some stories of his days as a midshipman on a Danish sailing ship.

One of his stories was about one period when they had been at sea for quite a stretch and the midshipmen complained to the number one that they were tired of the diet and needed fresh meat. The officer reminded them that they frequently had a fresh meat diet when they ate biscuits, which apparently were full of weevils. There is no doubt the King did not have any preferential treatment because he was a prince.

He also told us that when he was the officer on watch at a foreign port, a distinguished-looking man came aboard and questioned him about the prince who was a member of the crew. The King, noticing that he had not been recognized, just told some idiotic story that was supposed to relate to the actions of the prince, and later at dinner in the wardroom, the visitor realized he had been talking to the prince all the time.

This little episode apparently highly amused the King and the full story from the King's lips certainly tickled me.

When we arrived at Leeds, we were taken by car to Harewood House, the home of the Princess Royal and the Earl of Harewood. The King and his ADC stayed at the house, but I was found accommodation at the local inn, which belonged to the estate. (I think I mentioned earlier that a large part of Harewood House was being used as a convalescent hospital for officers.) I was staying just outside the park which contained the house, and walked to the house next morning. We then left for Richmond, where the King, who was the Honorary Colonel of the Green Howards, a famous Yorkshire regiment, was to be made the holder of the Freedom of the Borough.

We travelled to Richmond in the Earl's car and were driven by the Earl's driver. A few miles out of Leeds we were in collision with a truck being driven by a member of the 6th Airborne Regiment. It was a bleak and foggy day. Fortunately, nobody was hurt, but the right-hand side of our car was so badly damaged as to be unusable at our destination. The door handles were broken off and the mudguards completely ruined.

We were miles from a station or garage, so I asked the driver in charge of the convoy – who, by the way, was overawed when he discovered who the occupants of the car were, but he was put at ease by the usual friendliness of the King – to report the accident to the nearest police station or police officer, and at the same time ask the police to have a car meet us at Scott's Corner. We had made arrangements to take coffee at this spot. We continued our journey to Scott's Corner and shortly after we had consumed our coffee and other victuals, the replacement car arrived, much to the surprise of the King, who did not know of my actions at that time.

No comments were made and we proceeded on our journey to Richmond, where we arrived right on time. A procession was formed and the assembly walked through the ancient town, led by burghers with ancient staves, accompanied by the leading men and women of the town. After the ceremony of handing over the casket containing scrolls of the Freedom, we were all invited to take refreshments in the City Chambers.

The King was introduced to a newly arrived VC, a member of the Green Howards. I did not hear the conversation, but it must have been very amusing, because they constantly laughed loudly. After the ceremony we all adjourned to a local hostelry, where a very nice lunch was served. We returned to Harewood House later.

During the evening an inspector of the local police was awaiting my return. He had apparently decided to take some action against the driver of the truck. I assured him that this would not meet with the approval of the King, but of course I had no jurisdiction over the local police.

When I returned to the house next morning to accompany the King back to London, I was met by the Adjutant of the Green Howards, who had acted as liaison officer during this visit. He told me that I had been the subject of conversation at dinner the previous evening and the King had been full of praise for me. I was of course very pleased to hear what he had to say.

While we were travelling back to London on the train, I mentioned the conversation I had had the previous evening with the local police inspector. The King was very disturbed about the possibility of action being taken against the driver of the truck. He said, 'We owe these men so much and, after all, accidents can happen in peacetime, and this is war. What can I do to prevent it without interfering with normal justice?' I told the King that if he mentioned the matter to his ambassador, the matter could be dropped without the loss of face to anyone. This, I discovered later, was done.

Bill departed to Warrington about then, and he was soon back in his beloved Canada. By this time, we had managed to get Steve back near to us, because she was expecting to be moved to Canada at any moment. We fixed her up in lodgings at Reading, but of course needed to get her a little closer to us because we knew she would be leaving to take up residence in the far west of Canada.

We obtained accommodation of a sort in a local inn, the Prince of Wales, the landlord of which was a wartime friend of mine. The problem was to get Steve transported to the inn, but Raedar, never at a loss in these matters, suggested the King's Cadillac was the ideal method for the moving job, so one evening after we had returned from one of our trips to London, we set off for Reading.

It was nice having Steve near, but unfortunately this pleasure was not to last very long.

During the King's visit to London just about that time, we stayed in London during the night. The Chief liked to be on the spot to get first-hand news of the war and the Germans were then putting up some kind of resistance. The news was not too good, but the outcome of the war was not in any doubt at that stage of the fighting.

While we stayed at the embassy, the nights were frequently disturbed by the doodlebugs, which were still causing great damage and loss of life. At the same time the nights and days were interrupted by the terrific roar of the V2 rockets. They gave one a strange feeling because you could hear the rocket forcing its way through the atmosphere and the ultimate explosion before the explosion was visible to the eyes. Sometimes one could look into a beautiful blue sky with not a cloud in sight, then suddenly a small cloud would appear and just prior to its appearance, the roar of a rocket could be heard. In these cases of course the rocket had prematurely exploded in the sky.

On 18 February we visited Badminton, where the King took lunch with Queen Mary, and on the 22nd, after the usual meeting with the Storting at the embassy, the King lunched with officers of the American Red Cross in Golden Square. Once again I was able to enjoy some of the delicious food that I had partaken of many years before on American ships, together with double helpings of lovely creamy ice cream.

On the 24th, we visited the Duchess of Kent at The Coppings. The young Princess Alexandra and the young Prince George – now grown and public idols – were usually disporting themselves by sliding down the banisters of their home. They always seemed to be such friendly children.

On 1 March, we again journeyed to the docks, and after meeting the usual bunch of VIPs the King boarded a Norwegian cargo ship in the King George V Dock. Earlier in my career, as a member of the Special Branch, I had performed many hours of duty on these docks and as a consequence knew quite a lot of people engaged there, so I was happy to meet many old friends. The commander of the ship we boarded was also known to me, from an earlier visit with the King to Liverpool. I was also acquainted with the chief steward, so my lunch was a very satisfactory one and I came away with some extra smokes – quite a luxury during those difficult days. When we later went to Canada, this ship, with the same chief steward, called at Vancouver, and as I mentioned previously, I was not entirely forgotten, because the chief gave them a bottle – actually a magnum of champagne. So we were able to drink his health at a later date.

The beginning of March brought good news of the progress of the war, but sad news as far as Clarice and I were concerned. Steve received her 'marching' papers. Her movements were to be kept secret – in fact we knew nothing other than she was to go to London, where she would be met by Canadian authorities and retained in their charge for the time being.

On 7 March, I accompanied the King to London as usual. Before we left the house I told him that my daughter was leaving us for London and eventually would be transported to Canada. He arranged that I could be taken by the car to Waterloo Station at the time when Steve was due to arrive. Raedar and I arrived at the station, where we met Steve and Clarice. Our time together was very short, but we were able to carry the trunk to a waiting truck outside the station. It was a very sad but mysterious parting. We merely saw Steve placed in a covered truck, and from that time we were ignorant of what was going to happen. We merely surmised they would be taken to a reception centre and later shipped to Canada. So we had to content ourselves with hopes that her final journey would be a successful one.

About this time, the enemy submarines were concentrating round the coast of Britain, and a few were roaming the expanses of the Atlantic. From information I had gleaned from Norwegian skippers, I gathered that once a ship got clear of the 100-mile limit, her safety could be assured. Anyway, even with this information, we were both sick with worry and anxiety.

About three days later I was at the Yard when I met Harold Keble. He asked me if Steve had left and when I told him what had happened, he said, 'I would cease to worry, because I was at Greenock on the eighth of March to see some VIPs off and I noticed a ship lying in the river with a number of Canadian brides on board, and the ship left while I was there, so I presume Steve is well out in the Atlantic by now.' This information, together with the news of the latest activities of the U-boats, gave us a lot of reassurance.

Of course we did not entirely cease to worry until after we had received a letter from Steve confirming her arrival in Vancouver. Her letter was a breath of spring to us, because we also knew that Bill was safe and sound in Canada.

Life continued much the same as before and on 15 March, the King lunched at Lloyd's in Fenchurch Street. He had become a very popular individual by that time and there was quite a crowd present to greet him.

On the 16th he visited the Military Exhibition and we saw working models of the Mulberry Piers that were used in the landing at Normandy. On 1 April he again visited Rotherhithe Church. On 7 April, we attended the Cup Final between Millwall and Chelsea at Wembley. On the 9th we visited Westminster Abbey, where the King was conducted round by the Dean.

On 11 April, we left London for Glasgow, where we arrived next day at 7.15 a.m. After breakfast at the Central Hotel, we left at 11.00 a.m. for Neilston, where the King interviewed refugees. We returned to the hotel at 2.50 p.m. and at 4.00 p.m. went to the Seamen's Club in Vincent Street. An informal meal was served in the company of all those present, including many Norwegian seamen. The King made a speech and then at 9.00 p.m. we left Glasgow for Euston. On our arrival at Euston we proceeded to the embassy for breakfast and then stayed the night there, after the usual rounds.

We returned to Foliejon later the next day, but were back in London early the following day. We went to church at Rotherhithe on the 15th. On 17 April, the King, accompanied by the Crown Prince, attended the memorial service for Mr Roosevelt at St Paul's Cathedral. It was a very impressive service and attended by many members of the Allies and by members of the Royal Family. On the 25th the King again visited Westminster Abbey.

On the 28th we went to the Leicester Square Cinema. It was some special picture that the King wanted me to see, but I forget the name just now.

On 3 May 1945, we went to the Palace, where the King stayed for a while in discussion with the King and Queen.

On the 5th, he went to Bush House to make a special broadcast recording from 8.45 to 9.20 p.m. The end of the war was now imminent, so far as Europe was concerned; the Germans were in retreat on all fronts.

He went to the Connaught Hotel on 8 May to hear a broadcast to the nation by Mr Churchill, and later to Tavistock House to speak to some Norwegians.

On 9 May, VE Day, he paid a surprise visit to Mrs Smith, the widow of Lieutenant Commander Eric Smith.

It had been arranged that the Crown Prince, together with the Norwegian Government, should return to Norway and a ship was waiting in Glasgow Docks for this purpose. Raedar, who had purchased a good British motorcycle, was permitted by the Crown Prince to have it exported to Norway on this ship, which also took large quantities of Norwegian equipment.

On 11 May, we were in London again and stayed the night at the embassy. At 6.30 a.m. we went to King's Cross Station to meet the remainder of the Norwegian Royal Family – HRH Princess Martha and the two princesses and Prince Harald. After the usual greetings – very happy ones – we all proceeded to the embassy, where we stayed until the afternoon, and then to Windsor Castle, where we arrived at 4.00 p.m. They stayed for tea with the King and Queen and then left for Foliejon.

On 13 May, the Crown Prince returned to Norway on the *Devonshire*.

We attended church service on 15 May at Rotherhithe. It was good to see how the Norwegians present were excited to meet the children again. After church they all went to Buckingham Palace to lunch with the King and Queen. Later in the afternoon they all attended a special service at St Paul's from 3.00 to 4.30 p.m.

On 16 May to London again to make a special broadcast. On this occasion I misunderstood the orders and took the King to Bush House instead of Broadcasting House. The receptionist at Bush House, when spoken to by the King, mistook him for the King of Denmark. The King laughingly accepted her apologies when she discovered the mistake.

In the evening, the King attended the premiere of the film *The Three Sisters* at the Gaumont Cinema, Haymarket, then at 9.40 p.m. he went to the Admiralty, where he remained until 12.10 a.m.

On 17 May, Norway's Day, he attended a special thanksgiving service at St Paul's and at 11.00 a.m. a lunch given to Allied and British guests at the Dorchester.

We were in London for the next few days and the King was busy visiting many friends and VIPs before his departure for Norway.

The Norwegian Government were all, by this time, on their way back to Norway on the *Andes,* and the King received daily messages from the Crown Prince as to things in Norway.

On the 27th, he had a final luncheon date at The Coppings with the Duchess of Kent.

The last days of the King's wartime years in England were to be very hectic. He insisted upon meeting all his friends and associates before finally departing.

After lunching with the Duchess of Kent, he went to take tea with the British Royal Family at Windsor. The next few days saw the King in London, where he was kept busy purchasing presents and closing his affairs in England. During one of these visits, he purchased a lovely silver cigarette box and had the Royal Cypher engraved upon it. I did not know at the time of purchase that I was to be the recipient.

During the weekend, the King went for his usual walk round the park, accompanied by me, and on our return to the house, he asked me to come to his study. He gave me several folders of documents, which he instructed me to destroy – I had previously destroyed all secret documents for the King in the house furnace – and at the same time he presented me with the silver cigarette box and thanked me for my services. He said he would have liked me to accompany him back to Norway, but we both knew that my services would terminate as soon as he stepped aboard the vessel taking him back.

On 4 June 1945, we left Foliejon in the presence of many of the local inhabitants, who had become aware of his departure from Raedar, by that time a popular member of the local fraternity. To the shouts of good cheer and accompanied by Crown Princess Martha and the three children, we left the gates of Foliejon for good.

We went direct to the embassy and then to the Palace to say goodbye to the King and Queen.

In the afternoon at 3.00 p.m., the King went to Broadcasting House, Portland Place, to record a farewell message to the British people. In the evening the King was entertained to dinner by the Ambassador. While at dinner, the King's broadcast and part of a broadcast by Winston

Churchill were listened to with interest by the assembled guests.

At 9.45 p.m. the King left King's Cross, accompanied by the Crown Princess and his grandchildren. There was a large throng of Norwegians at the station to give them a rousing send-off. They flocked around the coach and it was with some difficulty that we finally departed.

The journey to Edinburgh was uneventful, but on our arrival there were more crowds to wish the King Godspeed. We drove direct to Millburn Towers, just outside Edinburgh, the lovely house which had been used by Norwegian officers during the war, where we had breakfast. Then we crossed by ferry to Rosyth, and there the King lunched with Admiral Whitworth at Admiralty House. The Admiral had served at Narvik, so was no stranger to the King.

From the windows of the house, one could see a great assembly of warships, including the *Rodney*, and many Norwegian flags were flying. A detachment of men of the Royal Marines provided the guard of honour when the King came to the quay. The Crown Princess and the children went aboard the *Norfolk*, the vessel that was taking the King back to Norway. The King inspected the guard of honour, then he came to me – shook my hand very heartily and thanked me for my services and said he hoped to see me again, but in Norway.

Admiral McGregor followed the King up the gangway to the bridge of the ship. The Norwegian flag on the aftermast was lowered, the Royal Standard being hoisted in its place, and the King's Admiral pennant went up at the peak. The *Norfolk* then slipped away from the quayside and signals were exchanged while the escorting fleet got under way.

The Norwegian *Stord* was in the lead, followed by three British destroyers, with the *Norfolk* and *Devonshire* bringing up the rear.

The Ambassador gave me a lift back to Edinburgh in his car and by the time we arrived at the ferry, the *Norfolk* was just passing under the Forth Bridge and the King could still be seen waving from the bridge.

On arriving back at Edinburgh, the Ambassador kindly drove me, at my request, to the headquarters of the city police. I said my goodbyes to members of that force who had assisted me very ably during the King's many visits to the North. I made a special point in thanking Bill Merrilees, Chief of the CID, who is now a Chief Constable of a Scottish borough.

I returned to London on the night train and went to the Yard to make my report early next day. I was later granted leave of absence for three weeks.

While enjoying my leave, I was able to think back on the last five years that I had been with the King, and how he was such a fine gentleman. He was very proud and behaved at all times as a king should. His thoughts were constantly with his people.

I reminisced about the time when we were due to leave for London to meet some dignitary and the King was suddenly troubled with a bad attack of lumbago, but this did not deter him from keeping the appointment. He must have been suffering untold agony. When he was due to alight from the car, he appeared to have difficulty in rising and I naturally went to assist him, but he declined my help in a graceful way and somehow got out of the car and immediately stood as erect as it was possible under the circumstances. On arrival back in the evening, he expressed the opinion that he had been abrupt with me, but said he felt it important to be an example to those around him, so he turned down my assistance on that account.

Once while we were coming past Windsor Station on the way home from London, Clarice emerged. She was going to catch the bus to the village. She nodded as the car went by, but the King evidently saw her and turned to me and said, 'Isn't that your wife, Coates?' On my replying in the affirmative, he said, 'Well, tell her to come along with us.' We stopped to pick up Clarice and she was invited to sit with the King. Social status was nothing to him – we were all human beings, some more fortunate than others.

During my time with the King, I was afforded many

opportunities which would have been denied me whilst performing ordinary duties. I was able to observe the conduct of all the members of the Royal Family and spent enjoyable hours at their various homes. I found them all very taciturn, but capable of smiling their appreciation. I was able to observe the mischievous Princess Margaret growing up and saw the present Queen fixing a wheel to an army truck during the difficult war years.

It was in all a very interesting period of my life and one I am always proud to look back upon.

12

Guests of the King of Norway

After my leave, I returned to ordinary duty once again, and the usual round of enquiries and meetings.

Towards the end of the year, the 'Governor' asked me to go to Gravesend with Harold Keble to start up Special Branch work, which had been dropped during the war years, when only war traffic was administered at this port. We were housed in the Custom House at Gravesend, and as the building had been badly damaged by enemy action, the office there was very cold and uncomfortable. There was, however, plenty to do and little time for sitting in the office.

We were daily boarding ships in the surrounding docks and at the various piers and almost every day one of us had to run down to Thameshaven to board a tanker. Smuggling in war materials was rife and various ways and means were being adopted to get the stuff into England, not by the normal smuggler but by members of the Allied forces, and quite a few officers were engaged in this pursuit.

We obtained a deal of information and passed it on to the Customs officers. The hiding places were many, but our information was perfect.

Then commenced the job of getting people back to their respective countries. Large numbers of Polish soldiers were being repatriated, having elected to return to their motherland. Care had to be taken to see that people did not take too much currency with them. Here again they tried all ways to defeat the authorities, but if we could find them out, it was a great achievement.

I used to mingle with the passengers when they arrived by train and sometimes their conversation led to the discovery of large sums of notes. Then there was the returning soldiery with their large bundles of Deutschmarks – almost worthless at that time.

On one occasion, I was checking passengers who were leaving on a boat for the Continent. For no apparent reason – merely suspicion – I had a naturalized Canadian under observation and asked Customs to give him a thorough search, but nothing incriminating was discovered. I was sure there was something wrong, so I phoned the Yard to have a search made, but again the answer was in the negative. I made a report and forwarded it to my boss. Three days later, a message was sent to 'All Ports' requesting that this man be arrested and detained for dealing in foreign exchange business. So my hunch was right after all. He did return, but through another port.

The winter came and it proved to be the worst the country had had for decades. We had a constant frost for seven weeks. The office with no heat was unbearable. We had, of course, to type out our reports there, and while doing so we would have our greatcoats on, and in spite of this we would constantly jump up and down and swing our arms. To anyone looking, it would have appeared that we were stark crazy.

When Steve left England, we had promised to come to Canada after the war to take up residence there, so about this time I was seeking ways and means of travelling to that country. Ships had not yet been released from war service, but this did not deter me from making enquiries from all my associates working in connection with ships. More of this later!

To return to the King of Norway.

After the King was back in Oslo and I had seen the film of

his arrival, I decided to write him a letter congratulating him on his reception. He, much to my surprise, answered my letter in his own handwriting, and that was the beginning of a series of letters between us, until just prior to his death in 1957. We exchanged views on the world situation and the King told me of the wonderful vessel the people of Norway had given him and of his forthcoming visit to the north of Norway.

At Christmas he sent me a Christmas card portraying the ship that the people had presented him with, *Norge*. He told me also of his experiences on his various visits – his letters were purely of a friendly nature, just one friend to another.

Early in 1946, the King asked me to spend my summer holidays with him in Norway. Of course I was delighted and honoured at this invitation, but was not too keen to leave Clarice alone in England. So when I wrote thanking the King for his kindness, I asked if it would be OK to bring my wife along. He replied to this letter by telegram, which said: 'I'm sorry that I did not make myself clear regarding the visit to Norway. I meant the invitation to include your wife.' In a subsequent letter he told me to get in touch with Sir George Ponsonby – this gentleman had been connected with the Norwegian Royal Family for many years and I had met him many times during the war. Sir George told me during a telephone conversation I had with him that he was making arrangements for the journey with the Norwegian Travel Bureau, and that all expenses were being covered by the King.

I knew most of the officials at Norway House, the London HQ of the Norwegian Travel Bureau, so I made an appointment with them. They drew up an itinerary so that Clarice and I could see some of the beautiful country; this made it necessary for us to stay one night in Bergen, for which they made arrangements. Feeling that these arrangements might not fit in with the King's plans, I wrote him a letter detailing everything. He replied at once and agreed with the plans and added, 'You will be able to get a glimpse of all sections of our lovely country.'

When I told the chaps about my invitation, they could hardly believe it. It was not long before a newspaperman came to interview me about the proposed trip and the events that led up to it, but thinking it would be against the wishes of the King, I refused to add to the story. This did not deter the men of the Press, so a news item on the front page of the *Express* the following day disclosed particulars of my coming visit to Norway.

Clarice and I duly set off for London on the arranged date – a taxi picked us up at the house and away we drove to King's Cross, where we boarded a train for Newcastle, travelling in style – it was a very strange feeling to be treated as a VIP.

On our arrival at Newcastle later that day, we were shown on board the MV *Astrea*, and conducted to a very nice deck cabin. We were both a little overwhelmed with the excitement of the day and the promised pleasures, so we retired to bed just after the vessel left her moorings and steamed down the river towards the open sea.

We awakened early next morning and after breakfast sat on the deck watching the various activities of the crew and other passengers. I conversed with some of the passengers – Norwegians whom I had met during my time with the King. The sea was calm and during the late afternoon, after we had passed some small Norwegian fishing vessels, we sighted land, and as the vessel got nearer to the shore, we were astounded at the beauty of the Norwegian coast – so rugged, but interspersed here and there with brightly coloured houses dotted all over the cliffs and in every little green hollow. We wondered how the people had managed to erect these delightful homes in such precarious spots.

It was late in the evening, still bright, that we rounded a rugged-looking cliff and entered the prettiest harbour I have ever seen. It looked as if all the villagers had come down to the harbour to welcome the vessel. We quickly discovered that we were in Stavanger.

Though a great friend of ours hailed from this lovely

town, we did not expect to see him there, so when we were told we could go ashore for the next three hours, we declined the offer. Shortly after this announcement, while looking over the side of the ship, we heard a voice that was very familiar to us both, that of Per, who had been the King's driver for a while in England and was one of the young Norwegians who had escaped from German domination by crossing the North Sea in a small fishing boat.

We had made arrangements to see him at Bergen, where he was in business, but he had decided to come to Stavanger and travel with us back to Bergen.

We went ashore and were greeted by Per's mother and father and other members of his family. Mrs Leversen presented Clarice with a beautiful bunch of flowers, and after a great welcome, we were driven to their home in the hills. I tried out my Norwegian and managed to carry on a conversation with them, and was almost overcome by their generosity and general attitude towards Clarice and myself.

After this memorable meeting, we returned to the ship and at midnight left for Bergen, travelling up the beautiful fiords and arriving early the following morning.

We were driven to the local hotel and then we paid visits to Per and later did a little shopping. Later in the day, Per took us on a round of the sights and showed us the German submarine harbours, then we had dinner at the hotel and so to bed.

Next day we left by diesel train from Bergen to Oslo, travelling over the mountains. This was the year of the Olympics and the train was full of people travelling to Oslo for the games. I knew many people on board and the journey was very pleasant, and there was no lack of enthusiastic Norwegians to point out the places of interest to us.

We stopped for a while in the mountains and here I was surprised to see a newspaper showing my photograph and a short piece about our visit to Oslo as guests of the King. I suspected Per had supplied the information and was a little perturbed about this.

We eventually arrived at Oslo at about 11.30 p.m. and here we were met by Raedar and a woman whom I thought at the time was his wife. She disclosed that she represented an Oslo newspaper, so I declined, as gracefully as possible, to talk. It was a waste of time on my part, because she said she was already in possession of the facts.

On leaving the station, we entered one of the royal cars which the King had sent to pick us up, and just as we entered the car someone took a flashlight picture of us. After a short journey we arrived at Bygdo Kongsgaarden, the King's Summer Palace. We were asked to wait in the entrance lounge by a manservant, who said the King would be with us in a moment.

After a few short seconds, the King came in and greeted us both very heartily. He said, 'You must be hungry, so come and eat and we can talk at the same time.' He accompanied us to a small dining room, where a meal was laid out. We sat and ate and talked most enthusiastically about events in general and especially the journey.

I told the King of the newspaper incidents and apologized for any comments and explained how I had endeavoured to keep things quiet. I was surprised to hear him say, 'That's all right – they are bound to get to know these things and, after all, we were together for so many years, and they are bound to connect your visit here with those days.'

We were subsequently shown to our room and on the following morning began a most interesting chapter of our lives.

Of course our visit was that of commoners, so we only came in contact with the King at his special request. I was commanded to speak to him later in the day and he told me arrangements had been made for us to be shown as much as possible in the short time at our disposal and he would like to see me now and again to make sure that everything was being done to make the visit a pleasant one. No effort was spared to make our trip one which would provide us with happy memories for life.

We visited the mountains and the fiords, the beautiful

stretch of water that fronts the City Hall of Oslo and then up into the valleys. We were shown spots on the rugged mountainsides where brave Norwegians had defended their country against the vastly superior German forces. We had a grand evening with Raedar and his wife up in the Valley Hotel.

The time went all too quickly.

On the eve of our departure from Oslo, we had an audience with the King. Clarice had a large bouquet of carnations to present to the King, but as usual she was too shy to say anything. I explained to the King that she was desirous of thanking him in her own words, but was overcome by his kindness. He replied, 'It is very kind of you both to honour me, but I'm the one who should do the thanking – you made life so much more bearable for me during the difficult days of the war, when my country was overrun by the enemy.

We were driven to the quayside, or Pipperviken, as it is called in Oslo, and after saying goodbye to Raedar, we boarded the Fred Olsen vessel *Bretagne* for England.

The journey down the Oslo fiord was lovely and we were able to view some more of the gorgeous scenery. As the vessel passed Drobak, a little village on the fiord, where we had been guests of a Norwegian retired sea captain, we were able to discern the captain and his wife waving and returned our greetings to them. They had their glasses trained on us until we were out of sight.

By the time we arrived in the open sea, it was time to retire, so we got into our respective bunks. Just as sleep was overcoming us, the ship started to roll and pitch, and I knew that we were in for a rough night. Clarice was soon out of her bunk and feeling sick. I accompanied her to the deck, but unfortunately she did not quite make it, and I was situated right in the wind. It was not long before we were both well and truly suffering from *mal de mer*. The sea was the roughest I had ever experienced – one small fishing vessel disappeared for several minutes at a time and just when we thought it had gone down, it would bob up like a cork.

We were very thankful to arrive eventually at Newcastle and by the time the ship had docked, we were feeling none the worse for our experience. The trip to London was uneventful after such a magnificent holiday. We were kept busy for weeks relating our experiences and they still remain most happy memories.

13

New Life in Canada

I carried on with the job at Gravesend and began to think I would soon have to take up residence there instead of travelling to and fro every day. I was still looking for a chance to get a berth on a vessel to Canada. The ships were still fitted out for transport of troops – ordinary passenger service had not then started, though many people were desirous of leaving England.

Winter came upon us and the last few months of that 1946–47 winter were really severe – the sea was frozen just off the east coast and it was most difficult travelling to work.

Late in April of 1947, I was informed by a friend working with the CPR shipping company that the Polish ship *Batory* was being fitted out for normal traffic after transporting troops to various parts of the world for the Allies. He said he could obtain passages for us on that vessel, but we would have to decide quickly. Clarice and I had a conference and decided forthwith to pack up and sail for Canada and another meeting with Steve and her family. The ship was due to leave on her first voyage as a passenger vessel from London to New York on 6 June. I immediately put the house up for sale and applied for my discharge from the police. My decision was a great surprise to all and sundry, but we carried it through. It was a very hectic time.

We had to get medically examined by the Canadian authorities and vaccinated to enable us to pass through the USA. Visas had to be obtained from the American authorities. Everything was accomplished in the time at our disposal and on the 6th we were duly ensconced on the *Batory* at Southampton.

The voyage started off badly with stormy weather and once again we were both sick. Clarice was very sick, but by the time we were in mid-Atlantic, we were both feeling in the pink. Arthur, our son, was not indisposed for one moment and in fact he had made many friends; when we eventually were able to sit on deck and enjoy the breezes, we were being introduced daily to Arthur's many acquaintances.

The ship arrived off the coast of America early in the morning and the sun was just peeping out as we passed the Statue of Liberty. I found the American Customs a bunch of mean officials, and it was late in the day before we were able to continue our journey.

As we were not due to leave New York until midnight, we checked our baggage and then went for a stroll through parts of the city. We all felt very ill at ease and decided that New York was a most unfriendly city. Clarice was badly in need of a cup of tea, something that had been denied her on the boat. We were fortunate in finding a café where a good cup of tea could be bought, and from that time, things were much more pleasant.

We were surprised to see what a terrific station Grand Central was, and how so much information could be gleaned from loud speakers and information bureaus. We found the checking of baggage a very simple but pleasant way of making travel most comfortable. The redcaps were a blessing. The rest of the day passed and we were not very impressed with New York – perhaps not a fair estimate, as we were only there for a short while.

After our first journey in a sleeper in America, we crossed the Canadian border in the early hours of the morning and our papers were examined on the train. We found the Canadian authorities both pleasant and helpful and the welcome they gave us was of great satisfaction after our initial treatment in New York. We were forced to remain in Montreal until late in the evening before we were able to leave for Vancouver.

Steve and Bill had asked Bill's uncle and aunt in Montreal to meet us and keep us company for the short stopover. On arrival at Montreal, I phoned Muriel and she arranged to meet us in a local hotel. We made our way there and she duly arrived and drove us with her husband round the beautiful city and to their lovely home. They supplied us with a grand Canadian dinner and then drove us to the station. Our first day in Canada had proved a very pleasant one and we were grateful for their kindness.

Late in the evening we boarded the train that was to take us across the wide expanse of the American continent. It proved to be a very eventful journey and the meals on the train were delightful and after the frugal meals that we had partaken of in England for the war years, the food seemed like magic. The scenes on the shores of Lake Superior were of most interest to me. It seemed very strange at that time to observe great ships in the middle of a continent. The journey across the prairie was a little dull, although we marvelled at the great stretches of wheat land.

The train stopped for a long stopover at Winnipeg and we took the opportunity of looking over this great city of the Middle West. At this time I was suffering with a great carbuncle on my elbow and was in need of something to ease it until I arrived in Vancouver. We had a quick look round the city and were very impressed with what we saw. During the train journey, I was assisting a passenger suffering with diabetes – he was unable to administer injections with his hypodermic needle because of the sway of the train, so I used to do it for him.

As we travelled on, we passed places with such interesting and romantic names as Moosejaw, and at once our thoughts went back to the days of the Indians and the Wild West. We later arrived in the Rockies and were astounded by the beauty of the majestic peaks. Our guide on the train enlightened us as to the names of the various mountains and described in detail the wonderful spiral tunnel. The journey from this stage was most interesting and my eyes were not closed for one second longer than necessary. The train winding its way along the banks of the mighty Fraser River is something to be remembered for ever. I had to think of the great skill and daring of the railway builders of the Great West.

In the early morning of Saturday, we drew into New Westminster and then eventually into Vancouver. The thrill of seeing Steve again was almost so overwhelming that I had the utmost difficulty in stopping tears from falling.

We found everyone most pleasant and our welcome was terrific. Vancouver seemed such a grand city and the surrounding country held great promise for exploration in the days to come.

After the preliminaries were over, we were driven to 4358 Union Street, and the pretty little house where Bill and Steve resided was most pleasing to behold. We were soon being introduced to many nice neighbours and the following days provided us with great pleasure.

After many days of bliss, I realized that money was an important thing in life in spite of the stories to the contrary. So I decided that I must get a job of some sort to augment my savings. My pension, I quickly discovered, was mere chickenfeed in a country that paid many dollars for a day's labour. Arthur soon got a job, but just as soon lost it. He did, however, succeed in getting something worthwhile, and as far as he was concerned, life on the American continent had started.

After many attempts I managed to get a small job with a large fish-packing concern, but this meant that I would have to leave home for a while. I took the chance of earning a little while I was getting acclimatized and within a few weeks was on my way to Kildonan, a small fishing hamlet on the west coast of Vancouver Island.

I caught the ferry to Nanaimo from the pier down at Burrard Inlet and two hours or so later I was roaming the small town. I found the boat for Kildonan and other outlandish spots was not due to leave until 6.00 p.m., so I entered a nearby café and partook of some raisin pie, the first I had ever tasted, and I must say it was delicious. Just before sailing time, or strictly speaking, departure time, because the small vessel was oil-driven, I made my way to the pier and met some of my fellow passengers, mostly loggers and fishermen returning to their respective camps. I quickly chummed up with a logger who was returning to work after several weeks in hospital as the result of an accident. I found my first real meeting with Canadians in the raw to be a very pleasant experience – they were most friendly and even offered me a drink from the bottle.

The trip up the inlet took quite a while and not one moment was lost in admiring the terrific scenery – coniferous trees of tremendous size, mountains and the odd bear fishing for salmon in the waters that we were travelling on.

We arrived at the pier at Kildonan after dark and I was met here by the manager – Mr MacKenzie. I discovered that it was the custom to allow many travellers who were going farther afield to stop over at the camp until the next boat arrived. There were five of us disembarked, and after being greeted by the manager, we were invited to his house to partake of refreshments. It was quite a party. I was later taken to the bunkhouse, which was over the offices and store. Here I was shown my bunk, a very comfortable affair, and I was also given instructions regarding meals, etc.

I discovered next morning that my bunk was surrounded by similar ones and the two nearest were occupied by a pleasant Canadian of Norwegian extraction and a Canadian of English extraction. They accompanied me to the 'grub' hut next morning. I found the table covered with great jugs of fruit juices and tomato juice and lashings of toast. I followed the example of the others and helped myself to two boiled eggs and after consuming these, was about to leave the table, but was surprised when I was told the eggs were merely a taster – the main breakfast was to follow, and what a feed! I was served by the Chinese cook with an enormous chunk of grilled ham, fried eggs and chip potatoes. I found it very difficult to swallow all this food, but discovered if I did not eat it, I would be looked down upon by my colleagues. After the meagre rations we had had in England, it was a difficult task, but I succeeded in cleaning my plate.

I then wandered round to the office, which was occupied by the manager and two other men – one the accountant and the other the bookkeeper. The whole camp was a series of huts built on piers and the office block consisted of the office, the store, where everything eatable and wearable could be purchased, and adjoining the store there was a commodious room which was used for concerts and a weekly picture show. I was allotted a small office which was rigged with a large 'send and receive' radio set. After a general run over the mechanics of the job I was to do, I commenced my listening-in work.

It was far from boring – the chatter from the various vessels plying their jobs many hundreds of miles out in the ocean I found to be most interesting and very enlightening. I even learned how the fishermen could 'smell' out the fish by the colour of the water. In between fishing they would discuss the latest news and sports results.

After the morning had passed very quickly, I set off for my midday meal – another great feast, steak, potatoes and veg followed by great chunks of pudding and washed down by lovely large cups of American-style coffee.

This pleasant state of affairs lasted all the week, but on Saturday and Sunday we were allowed to roam around the camp and exchange pleasantries with one another. I discovered Kildonan to be a very nice and happy community of men – there were just two women living there, the doctor's wife and the wife of the manager.

On Sunday morning I went to explore the reservoir at the top of the nearby mountain, which was only accessible by climbing a track with the aid of a rope suspended from rails on the side. I was always fond of wandering about, so I eventually found myself at the top of the mountain on a large expanse of scrubland. In the distance I thought I observed a woman and a small child picking berries, so feeling in need of a little companionship, I wandered over, but much to my surprise I discovered the 'woman and child' to be a black bear and its cub. I did not stop to investigate further, but chased like hell down the track back to camp.

I arrived breathless and very scared at the camp, where I met Ola the Norwegian. When I told him about the incident, he laughed his head off. He later reassured me that bears were not unduly dangerous, so long as you did not interfere with their cubs. I found this statement to be quite true, because I saw many bears and was very close to them in the ensuing weeks.

In the evening we had a wiener roast by a terrific log fire on the shore of the inlet. I was thrilled with this type of living and wished I had discovered it years before. I used to sit in the evening on the boat rails chatting to the fishermen about things in general. There were quite a lot of Indians bringing fish to the camp. Fish was bought and ice supplied from the factory. The camp contained a canning plant, but no canning was being done during my stay. Two or three young university students worked at stacking fish. They went to the camp during their vacations to obtain money for the furtherance of their studies. One of them had travelled the length of the North American continent by hitching a lift. He entertained us at times with some very interesting anecdotes.

We became chummy with the son of the Fishery Inspector, who used to deputize at times for his father. He invited us to take evening trips up the inlet on several occasions and I found them very enjoyable. We explored many old Japanese fishing camps that had become overrun. They had been taken from the coast when the Japanese came into the war against America.

One evening when we were on one of these trips, the fuel tank sprang a leak and the bilge became saturated with the gasoline, a very dangerous situation which we had to remedy very quickly for fear of an explosion. We could not make a landing because the shore was too rugged, so we considered collecting most of the bilge water and throwing it together with the leaky tank, overboard. After consultation, we decided against this because of the danger of floating gasoline on the surface of the water in a shipping lane. Large ships frequently passed down the inlet – laden with timber – on the way to the open sea.

We discovered a floating hulk of an old Indian canoe, so we manoeuvred our vessel close to this hulk and dumped, as best we could, all the waste and the tank into this hulk. This still constituted a danger, so we decided to endeavour to ignite the stuff; our efforts in this direction were most amusing, because owing to the rush of water, it was impossible to draw up alongside, so we each took a turn at throwing lighted waste into the hulk, and after some minutes we succeeded in igniting the fuel. There was a loud rush of air and flames shot high into the air, but at the same time we drove the boat as far off as possible.

Just after we had cleared off, a large vessel came down the inlet laden with timber. We were by this time a little scared as to the result of our actions, which seemed a little unorthodox, but the only ones under the circumstances. The large vessel hove to for a while – they probably thought there was someone in distress – but after a short investigation the vessel resumed its journey. We all arrived back at camp feeling a little frightened, but said nothing and the incident became a thing of the past very quickly. It was, however, exciting while it lasted.

My job at Kildonan was only of a temporary nature, so it was not long before I was back in Vancouver. The outfit had promised to fix me up with a job in town, but just at that period they were suffering a recession, so I had to start looking for something else to do.

In the meantime, we decided to purchase a house. Clarice was about to fall in love with a romantic house on Capitol Hill with a Spanish flavour, but we discovered our mistake before we had fully committed ourselves, although not before I had lost $250 as a deposit. I had been well and truly caught that time.

We did eventually manage to buy a nice old house at Pender Street, and very soon established ourselves there with brand-new furniture. The buying of furniture for this house I am sure gave Clarice one of the greatest thrills of her life.

I soon began to look for a job, but not with much success. I made several calls on likely possibilities, but found the prospective employers just as big liars as those we meet in England. I did, however, meet General Clark, a local lawyer for whom I did some work. It was just a temporary job, but he tried to get me fixed up with many local firms. Again, however, it was difficult because of the setbacks that seem to hit Vancouver during the winter months.

Just before Christmas, as the result of General Clark's efforts, I became a shop detective at Spencers in Hastings Street. I had some success here, but after making many friends amongst the people employed there, I discovered the job was again only a temporary one, and in the new year I was again out of a job. I tried my hand at divorce work with a local detective agency, but though the money was good, I disliked the idea of snooping, so gave it up. I was offered a job as house detective with the Vancouver Hotel, but the union rules forbade my employment because I was not a member.

My bad luck did not last much longer, because at the beginning of February, I had an interview with Charlie Block-Bauer at Marpole Woodyard, a subsidiary of the Eburne Saw Mills. The interview was at 11.00 a.m. on a Monday and at 12.00 noon, I was starting on a job which was to prove most congenial for the remaining few years in Canada. I quickly made friends with everyone there and everything was most pleasant.

After the first year I bought myself a new car – the first I had ever had. We had many trips down to the States and visited Seattle, and one weekend we went to Mount Baker. The terrific heights scared me and I was glad that Fred Kirkman, a friend and neighbour of ours, was present to take the wheel. We had many rides in Bill's old jalopies – trips to Boundary Bay, Deep Cove, etc. I found the scenery most enchanting and could have stayed there for the rest of my life.

Bill and Steve moved from Union Street into a lovely new house on Gilmore and we had the boys, Brian and Alan, up to visit us daily, and of course found the telephone a very important part of our daily life.

Life was then one long bliss, but this could not last for ever. Unfortunately Bill – not, of course, unfortunate for Bill – was transferred to Seattle, which meant our almost co-existence was at an end. Steve and Bill were quickly followed by our friends Danny and Lucille, then George and Estelle took the plunge, and in a very short time, we were all separate once again.

We visited Steve and Bill on many occasions, but these visits did not make us any happier. Clarice became a different woman, and although we travelled the length and breadth of the States and even into Alberta, I could see that Clarice was unhappy. She became sick with blood poisoning and to remedy this we went down to Utah. While there, on the advice of the doctor, we bathed in the Great Salt Lake. It proved a tragedy in a way, because Clarice suffered agony through the briny water – we almost turned back, but she recovered and we spent the rest of the vacation visiting California and other places of interest.

The following year, Clarice became sick again and this time the doctor said she was suffering as a result of nostalgia for England.

That summer we had a lovely trip down to Los Angeles with Steve and Bill – the boys spent their vacation on a ranch. While we were at Danny's place, my car was kept in cold storage, but we travelled in Danny's car to Las Vegas. Here Bill almost won a packet. However, it proved a very interesting holiday and the later trip to San Diego and the race track at Hollywood Park, where Bill and Danny won handsomely, enabled us to have a grand fling in Los Angeles before returning to Seattle and Vancouver.

On our way back from Santa Monica, we called to visit friends in Santa Barbara and later that night arrived in Salinas, in the centre of the States' vegetable-growing country. We soon were accommodated in a very nice auto court and later toured the town to eat and then went to bed.

Our start early next day took us along the coast and the weather was not too good – it was heavy with fine rain and visibility was down to about 50 yards. The rest of the journey to Seattle was wet, so we decided to make for home as quickly as possible.

When we arrived at one stop – I forget where just now – the rain was coming down so hard that I was unable to see the front of the car, so we were forced to stop and seek shelter at once. We duly arrived back at Seattle all in one piece, and after a pleasant night with Steve and Bill we resumed our journey to Vancouver.

The following year we went with the Martins (friends of ours) to Radium Hot Springs and Banff, and after climbing Sulphur Mountain at Banff (for which Clarice received a certificate), we left for Fort MacLeod and later crossed the border at Sweetgrass into Montana. We toured Montana and visited Virginia City, and then had a final night at Helena. Shortly after our return to Vancouver, I began to make arrangements for returning to England.

I put our house up for sale – it seemed for a while that there were no buyers, but eventually it went. I made arrangements to sail on the *Empress of France* in late September. We then went to stay with Belle and John (Steve's in-laws) at Commercial Drive. Our holidays we spent with Steve and Bill – we travelled by train, as I had already sold my car.

We spent the last month with Steve and Bill at Seattle. I well remember the last job I did there was to help paint the house. I had to return to Vancouver to wind up everything and then went back to Seattle for the last few days.

I was dreading the time for leaving to arrive, but it came one bright day, when life in Seattle can be so pleasant. I felt very depressed when the farewell came. Bill drove us to the station and, accompanied by the boys and Steve, we waved goodbye. It was suggested that Steve, Bill and the boys should wave at us as the train passed by Golden Gardens. We chose Golden Gardens because Bill and the boys and I had spent many pleasant hours down there. But unfortunately when the train reached the spot, we got only a fleeting glimpse of them.

One Sunday morning when we were playing with the boys on the sands, Alan, while looking for the ball we were playing with, came across the body of a woman who had obviously drowned. It was a very unpleasant sight, but somehow quickly forgotten by all.

The trip across the States in the *Empire Builder* was very interesting, but I was still feeling very unhappy and I remained very discontented for several years after.

At Chicago we had about ten hours to wait for the Toronto connection, so we explored the city of the Middle West. Some of the street scenes were very frightening to Clarice, but we managed to find our way to a lovely spot by Lake Michigan. We could hardly believe that such a great expanse of water was really a lake.

On our return to the main station, we boarded a train for Montreal. It was late and very dark, so we were unable to see much of the surrounding country. The train was not nearly as comfortable for travelling as the one we had left in Chicago. We saw Toronto in the light, but arrived at Montreal in the dark. However, we managed to get a place to stay the night. We wandered downtown and saw some more of that great city, where French is spoken by almost everyone and the very buildings and streets are of French architecture.

On our arrival in our cabin on board the *Empress of France* we were greeted with a bouquet of lovely flowers and telegram from Steve and Bill. This helped to make me feel a little happier. It was a beautiful day as we sailed down the St Lawrence and we were able to observe some of the beautiful scenery. By the time we reached Quebec, the night darkness had fallen, but the twinkling lights of that ancient city looked lovely from the deck of the ship.

The following day was still bright and warm, but the barren coast of Labrador made one feel very cold at times. We passed the famous Belle Isle – previously know to us through the famous murder case of Dr Crippen. It was dusk when the vessel was well out in the open sea – then we suddenly saw a great iceberg on the port side. Shortly afterwards the ship began to rock and Clarice began to look a little green. We were at dinner at the time, but she did not feel like continuing, so we retired to our cabin. Arthur was, however, enjoying himself with the other passengers.

In the morning, Clarice felt much better and we walked the deck for a while, breathing in the lovely clean air. Nothing could be seen either on the port or starboard side, nor ahead.

That evening we were overwhelmed with the beauty of the sight of the Aurora Borealis – never to be forgotten. The next few days were just the usual shipboard ones – the odd game of bingo and horse racing, etc.

14

Home Again

One dark night, we arrived off the coast of Ireland and the lights from the distant shore were a very welcome sight. We looked at these for some time, then returned to our cabin and quickly fell asleep.

In the early hours of the next morning we awoke to see the shores of England and it appeared very soon that the ship was alongside the jetty at Liverpool. We were quickly onshore and the Customs clearance was soon over – having been assisted very ably by a friend of Alan MacQuarrie's. The train journey down to Bristol was a little monotonous and how strange everything seemed. I felt that I had been away from England for years – the trains looked like toys and the fields were like a jigsaw puzzle. The only thing that reminded us of the last few years was the sight of the Hereford cattle as we passed through Hereford.

It was dark when we arrived at Bristol, where we were met by Clarice's sister Madge and husband Court. A good hot cup of tea made us all feel much better, and a swig of the rum I had bought on the ship assisted still more. We spent the next few days renewing our acquaintanceship with our many friends there and then decided it was time to visit my kinfolk. The next few days found us far afield in Worthing one day, Brighton the next and in Kent and down to Dover.

I had a few days in London, and of course visited my old colleagues in the Branch at Scotland Yard. We returned to

Bristol and then began the usual scouting for a job. The prices of articles in the shops had increased beyond my imagination and my pension was much too small to permit me to just languish, so it was job-seeking all over again. If I had been living in London, the opportunities would have been great, but Clarice had set her heart on living in Bristol, so I had to make the best of it.

My one big handicap was the fact that I knew nobody of any consequence, and in a world where it is who you know and not what you know that counts, I could see I was going to be faced with tremendous difficulties. This did not deter me and I made applications at all the likely places. In some I got as far as an interview and in one case got on the short list, but nothing but promises resulted. December came and still I was unplaced, but on the first day of that month, I saw an advert in the local press and wrote the usual letter. Much to my surprise, I received a reply and in due course got a job with the Gloucestershire Territorial Association as a clerk. This job was connected with administration work with the Territorial Army, and I was appointed to do that kind of work with an artillery regiment, the 312 HAA Regiment. This was very interesting, because many years before I had been a member of an artillery regiment and had at that time performed some similar duties.

Unfortunately, soon after I had commenced this new job, the government started an economy drive and the regiment to which I was posted for duty was to be disbanded, so in a very short time, I was to be out of work once again. For the next few months, I was busy winding up the affairs of the regiment, and just when I was due to sign on at the local labour exchange, I was invited to join the new regiment – 311 – to do similar work. I naturally jumped at the opportunity. Work went merrily on for the next few years and then in 1960 the axe fell again. Fortunately by this time I had got outside the 'new entrants' ring and stood a chance of securing another job with a new outfit.

I was duly posted to my present regiment – 341 Signal Squadron – but did not commence work with this unit until

I had wound up the old regiment. It seemed to me that I was getting all the important jobs but not improving my status at the same time. However, I was not unduly perturbed about the turn of things. So long as I had a job, I was satisfied.

It seemed disappointing that with all my abilities for a good security job, the fact that I was not known in the district prevented me from obtaining a job more in keeping with my skill. Age was winning the argument and I have now given up the struggle. I have been assisted in this way of thinking more by the severe cuts in my income by tax than anything else. It seemed fruitless to work hard only to give the rewards for labour back to the government to throw away on hare-brained schemes.

Though I have not achieved the things I would have liked in the past few years, I have been fairly contented and have visited a large number of places in the British Isles.

Every year I have been to camp with the regiment and this enabled me to visit interesting spots like North Wales, South Wales, Pembrokeshire, Portsmouth, Salisbury Plain, Dartmoor and Folkestone. I have always stayed in lodgings at these places and have met many interesting people and have thus broadened my mind. In addition, Clarice and I have spent pleasant vacations in Scotland, England and even in Germany. This latter visit was an interesting experience. We were able to meet Arthur's in-laws for the first time, and with my slight knowledge of the German language, I was able to converse with the inhabitants and in so doing made many friends and met some very nice people.

This period was also one to be remembered because of the visit for a long vacation of Steve and our youngest grandson, Scott. It was indeed a great moment when we met for the first time at London Airport – Heathrow.

The last seven years has also brought tragedy into our lives. The death of my oldest brother was a sad blow and then this was followed by the death of my mother. Thus a link with the past was broken for ever. I was so happy to know that Steve was able to visit her granny before the old lady died. They were always very fond of each other.

I think this is a good time to conclude this story of my life, even though I hope to remain on this good earth for many years to come. Though I have not achieved the things I would have liked to have done, I still remain very contented with life, and have only one regret, and that is that we are so far from our young kinfolk.

Life is something that we control ourselves, with one big exception – some have plenty of luck and others never quite make the grade. This is, even so, a small detail so long as one has good health.